There are many danger areas in life where a passion for something God-given can take over from our passion for God – and body image is one of them. This timely book sets out to help us find – and keep – a healthy balance.
*Rosemary Conley, CBE*

This book could change your life! It will take you behind the behaviours with which you struggle – and the behaviours with which you ought to struggle – to the underlying causes. Not only does this bring hope for change, but it brings hope for gospel change – change that is good news. The diagnostic helps alone are worth the price of the book!
*Tim Chester, author and a leader of The Crowded House, Sheffield*

Julian Hardyman has given us a gripping and deeply perceptive treatment of this subject. His book speaks powerfully to the greatest danger of the Christian life and combines uncompromising challenge with personal honesty and pastoral compassion. It is a book of warning and hope, an alarm and a call to battle. It should be on every church bookstall – and quoted from the pulpit too!
*Peter Lewis, author and pastor, The Cornerstone Evangelical Church, Nottingham*

JULIAN HARDYMAN

GOD'S BATTLE
FOR OUR HEARTS

ivp

INTER-VARSITY PRESS
Norton Street, Nottingham NG7 3HR, England
*Email: ivp@ivpbooks.com*
*Website: www.ivpbooks.com*

*First published 2010*

**British Library Cataloguing in Publication Data**
A catalogue record for this book is available from the British Library.

ISBN: 978-1-84474-418-3

Set in Monotype Dante 12/15pt
Typeset in Great Britain by CRB Associates, Potterhanworth, Lincolnshire
Printed and bound in Great Britain by Ashford Colour Press Ltd, Gosport,
Hampshire

*Inter-Varsity Press publishes Christian books that are true to the Bible and that
communicate the gospel, develop discipleship and strengthen the church for its mission
in the world.*

*Inter-Varsity Press is closely linked with the Universities and Colleges Christian
Fellowship, a student movement connecting Christian Unions in universities and colleges
throughout Great Britain, and a member movement of the International Fellowship of
Evangelical Students. Website: www.uccf.org.uk*

To my parents,
Norman and Carol Hardyman,
and my parents-in-law,
Les and Pam Manderson

# CONTENTS

# ACKNOWLEDGMENTS

I would like to thank the elders and members of Eden Baptist Church for the study leave periods in July 2006 and from April to June 2009 during which this book was written, as well as for their support and prayers, particularly through my five months of sick leave in 2006. Special thanks are due to Marvin Wong, my dear friend and colleague, who shouldered the leadership of the church during this second sabbatical (as he did heroically during my illness).

Abundant thanks to Gabriel and Olwen Laszlo for letting me stay in their home in North Wales for a week's solitary writing overlooking a stunningly beautiful lake.

The work of a group of American Presbyterian leaders and writers has massively shaped my thinking on idolatry: Elyse Fitzpatrick, Tim Keller (whose then unpublished material has been seminal), Jack Miller, David Powlison and Paul Tripp. I have learned so much from them. I have tried in the text to acknowledge my debt to them, but really the whole book is an introduction to their powerful exposition of idolatry (for more details see the 'Further reading' section, p. 215). Interactions with Jenny Dorsey and Tim Chester have proved instructive too. Others who have helped with material and encouragements include Peter Lewis, Ro Mody and Dan Strange. The Eden congregation heard the sermons where much of this material first saw the light of day; Judith Taylor first encouraged me to try to publish it.

Many thanks to the wonderful team at IVP, notably Kate Byrom whose thoughtful suggestions have greatly improved my efforts. I also deeply appreciate Bryony Benier's expert copy-editing. Being published by IVP is a huge privilege for me. Amy Donovan's comments have also greatly improved the text at several places and her help in tracking permission to quote Bruce Springsteen was indispensable.

Special thanks are due to my family: my wonderful children, Robin, Fiona and Kitty, and Debbie, my beloved wife, who challenges my pet idols, inspires me to put Christ back in his rightful place in my heart and goes on loving me when I'm impossible to live with.

This book is dedicated to my dear parents, Norman and Carol Hardyman, and my dear parents-in-law, Les and Pam Manderson. Their love and support for my life and ministry through good times and hard ones means more to me than I can say. My father – a supremely gifted wordsmith and master of the telling understatement – died while the book was being written. His example continues to inspire me. When I was struggling to complete the book I remembered his oft-repeated injunction, an attempt I think to reduce the length of my sermons, 'Julian, if you leave it out, they'll never know.'

I am grateful to friends who challenge me: you can read about one of them in chapter 1. While I was in the early stages of writing this book, another challenged me to consider whether perhaps I was making writing it into an idol. Such bold love is a precious gift (Proverbs 27:6) and it drives me to express the hope that this book will be all for the glory of Almighty God, Father, Son and Spirit, whose name is Jealous, whose being is glorious and whose passion is to get our hearts back. For himself.

Julian Hardyman
Cambridge, June 2009

# INTRODUCTION:
# GOD'S BATTLE FOR OUR HEARTS

When my girlfriend and I had been going out for a few months we hit a rough patch. She was taking her dentistry finals and needed to focus on toothy exams. I was unsympathetic. When I wasn't the centre of her attention every weekend, I got angry and depressed in rotation. She seemed more interested in molars than me: my mood dived.

It reached the point where we were almost splitting up. Things came to a head one weekend when I had to fly off to Amsterdam on business. I remember wandering round the Van Gogh museum (not the most cheerful of settings) on the verge of tears. From the hotel, I rang an older Christian friend and arranged to go round to see him when I got back from the Netherlands. I warned him why I was coming.

## In Jesus' place

When I arrived at his house, we sat down with a cup of tea (the British approach to pastoral care) and I began to open up. He listened carefully and asked a few questions. Then he said, 'Julian, I wonder if She has become more important to you than Jesus.'

I instantly realized it was true. I had made Her more important to myself than Him. I had started to invest in Her all my hopes for happiness and security, rather than in my Lord. I realized that *this* was the reason why I was so depressed and angry.

Afterwards my friend shared that he had been planning to say the usual comforting words, but that as I came through the door of his house, the Lord seemed to prompt the words which – rather nervously – he spoke.

That was my first real insight into what I would now call *idolatry*: putting anything else in the place that is rightfully God's and his alone – and then suffering the consequences. Now this may seem very remote from your life: after all, an idol is like a garden gnome and you don't have any garden gnomes, let alone worship them, do you?

## It's not just me

Since then, as I have read and preached the Bible and listened to people describe their lives, I have seen again and again how idolatry explains us and our problems. I have also found that God is deeply committed to turning us from our idols, at conversion and then progressively throughout our Christian lives, so we will worship him alone. God takes this so seriously that he has committed himself to fight a war to make it happen. That is what this book is about.

## A tale of a city

Imagine a walled town in Tuscany, Italy, in, say, the fifteenth century. It belongs to the Duke of Florence. Normally it is a quiet, peaceful place. The market place is bustling with stalls selling olive oil, huge whole dried hams, pungent (but delicious) cheeses, ruby red wine and crusty bread. On most days children run through the streets chasing puppies and bowling hoops. Today is different. The place is full of soldiers and the townspeople are indoors. The Duke's arch-enemy, the Duke of Pisa, has marched up unexpectedly over the mountains, breached the walls with the help of traitors, and captured the town. Like many Italian towns of the day, it has many towers.

The Pisan troops have taken up defensive positions in each and every one. Their flag is now flying from the highest tower. They are in control.

### Under siege

What does the Duke of Florence do? He summons his soldiers and marches to lay siege in his turn until he has recaptured his beloved town and repossessed it. Even after the Florentine troops have got through the city walls and secured the market square, they still have to take back each of the towers one by one. It is a gradual process, but they know they will succeed in the end.

### God wants your heart back

Your heart is that town. It has been captured, but God wants it back. He is engaged in a war to recapture your heart, tower by tower, from the idols you have invited in to rule it.

## I don't have idols!

In Ezekiel 14 people come to God for help, but he tells them that they have idols in their hearts.

> These men have set up idols in their hearts and put wicked stumbling-blocks before their faces.
> (Ezekiel 14:3)

It's like when you go out and buy a new TV and carefully set it in the right position in your lounge. That's what they've done with the idols: they've set them up in their hearts.

### What idols?

When we hear the word 'idol' we tend to think of football players or pop stars. *Pop Idol* on TV is all about trying to find new singers or groups to become 'idols'. Celebrity culture is a bit tacky, but surely that can't be the problem with our lives.

We may even remember that some people's religion meant worshipping idols: little or large statues that represented a god (and may even have been thought to be the god by some). And at that point we may think, 'Well, I like music and football, but I don't idolize Wayne Rooney or the Sugarbabes; I certainly don't worship the gnomes in my garden.'[1] So what's the problem?

### Beatle idols

When George Harrison, the Beatles' guitarist, died in 2001 many of his friends paid tributes to him. One described Harrison's kindness to him when he had been ill. He said that Harrison came to his hospital bed carrying a present. It was a small brown Hindu statue. 'He'll look after you,' said Harrison and left it on the window sill. It was an odd reminder of what idolatry looked like: investing hope in a carved image.

### Idols of many kinds

Very few of us would invest our hopes in little statues. So are we idol free? Not at all. The Bible used the picture of idolatry as a way of describing anything that takes the place of the true God in our lives. Not depictions of the Greek goddess of love Aphrodite, but mental images of naked bodies. Not literal temples where we go to worship real statues, but inner urges for more and more. Not stone altars to sacrifice on, but bragging about the money in the bank and the turnover of the market stall. It's all idolatry: putting something else in God's place.

That's why John finishes his first letter with this terse reminder: 'Dear children, keep yourselves from idols' (1 John 5:21).

### Idolatry today

In Bible times (as in some cultures today) idol worshippers took offerings of food and drink to the temple. They presented them to their idols, thinking they would please them with choice things. Idolatry today isn't going to the British Museum and putting a Mars Bar in front of a little clay statuette that an archaeologist dug up in Syria. Idols are not just on pagan altars, but in well-educated hearts. Idols are not just in ruined temples, but in modern homes and offices. The question is not whether you have idols or not. The question is whether you recognize them.

## Get real about those idols!

### Idol factories and idol altars

Idols are our biggest problem; we will never understand ourselves or God's grace to us, unless we grasp how our hearts constantly create and worship idols. They are idol factories because they work round the clock making idols out of things God has given us.[2] They become altars where we offer those idols our best energies and our deepest devotion and our highest trust. Every single human being does this: we worship the gifts, not the Giver, and in doing so we destroy ourselves. Understanding this is the key to understanding who we are. Understanding God's response is of immense importance – a powerful, liberating and positive experience for us.

As we understand idols and how they work, we find out a great deal about ourselves. Why we get so angry about traffic jams. What drives us to work so hard that our marriage hits the rocks. What lies behind that compulsion to look at pornography. Why you feel irrationally depressed when you fail to have a prayer time one day. Why not being asked to lead your house group Bible study leaves you so resentful.

Most important of all, we see what it is that seduces us away from drinking the living water of God's salvation.

### God's surprise

Remember those Israelite people in Ezekiel? God would have had every reason to send them packing: he answers them in the most appropriate way. What do you think that would be? Rejection? Destruction? Telling them to back off and go back to their problems? No – he announces a plan driven by love *to get those hearts back again*.

> I will do this to recapture the hearts of the people of Israel, who have all deserted me for their idols.
> (Ezekiel 14:5)

'Recapture' is a military word. Go back to that Tuscan town, captured by the enemy; their hated flag is flying over it. The king hears the news, raises a new army, travels across country, lays siege to the city and pours his efforts into recapturing it. That's what God is saying he will do to these people's hearts.

### He's after your heart

This book is about a military campaign. I want to show you that God is at war and he is fighting for your heart. You are like the town that has been captured by the enemy – idols – and God is throwing everything he's got into recapturing your heart for himself. He has devoted 'all [his] heart and soul' (Jeremiah 32:41) to getting you back. He has engaged in the greatest war of cosmic history. It puts the Hundred Years War, the Punic Wars, the Second World War, or even the fictional Star Wars all into the shade. This is a War for the Glory of God in the hearts of men and women. Including yours.

*Love on the rocks?*
What happened to the relationship I described earlier? As it worked out, Debbie and I got married nine months after my Amsterdam crisis. But the most important effect of my friend's brave words was to restore my relationship with Christ. And God's battle to recapture my heart continues.

He wants yours too.

## For discussion or personal reflection
Read Ezekiel 14:1–6.

1. God's great concern is with idolatry: what does that tell us about his plan for those people's lives?
2. How do you feel about this being true of you too?
3. What does your heart need to be recaptured from?
4. How do you think God goes about doing this?
5. Why is verse 6 important?
6. Why not use this verse from a well-known hymn to tell God what you want to do with your idol(s):

> The dearest idol I have known,
> Whate'er that idol be,
> Help me to tear it from thy throne,
> And worship only thee.[3]

# PART ONE

# WHO HAS IDOLS ANYWAY?

# 1. IDOL DIAGNOSIS

What are *my* idols then? By now some people will be anxious that they have a shelf-full, some not at all sure they have any, and others thoroughly confused.

## Quick review

Let's review what we have learned about idols. Idols are anything or anyone we put in the place of God in our hearts – and therefore our lives. What does that mean?

Martin Luther, who was alive to the dangers of idolatry in his day, gives a powerful definition:

> A god is that to which we look for all good and in which we find refuge in every time of need. The trust and faith of the heart . . . make both God and idol . . . That to which your heart clings and entrusts itself is really your God.[1]

This can happen in many different ways.

## Thirteen varieties

David Clarkson suggests thirteen acts of 'soul worship' that should belong to God, but which idolaters give to their idols:

- Esteem – that which we most highly value.
- Mindfulness – that of which we are most mindful (i.e. think about the most).

- Intention – that at which we most aim.
- Resolution – that about which we are most resolved.
- Love – that which we most love.
- Trust – that which we most trust.
- Fear – that which we most fear.
- Hope – that for which we most hope.
- Desire – that which we most desire.
- Delight – that in which we most delight and rejoice.
- Zeal – that for which we are most zealous
  (i.e. enthusiastic, passionate, committed).
- Gratitude – that to which we are most grateful.
- And finally: 'When our care and industry is more
  for other things than for God – this is idolatrous.'[2]

There's a story about Chris Evert in her pomp. She had just marmalized one of life's quarter-finalists and, when they were both in the locker room, the beaten one announced in a loud, meant-to-be-overheard voice, 'Thank God my happiness doesn't depend on winning a tennis match.' Evert responded equally loudly, 'Thank God mine does.'[3]

Now that doesn't mean we can't love our neighbour, trust our business partner or desire our husband. It is a matter of where we invest our ultimate love or concern, of who comes first for each of these. Idols are rivals to God.

## What it looks like when it's walking towards you
Clarkson gives some examples of practical idolatry in his sermon:

When you are more careful and industrious to please men or yourselves, than to please God – when you are more careful to provide for yourselves and posterity, than to be serviceable unto God – when you are more careful as to what you shall eat, drink, or be clothed, than how you may honour and enjoy God – when you are more industrious to promote your own interests, than the designs of God – when you are more careful to be rich, or great, or respected among men, than that God may be honoured and advanced in the world – when you are more careful how to get the things of the world, than how to employ them for God – when you rise early, go to bed late, eat the bread of carefulness [i.e. anxiety], that your outward estate may prosper, while the cause, and ways, and interests of Christ have few or none of your endeavours – this is to idolize the world, yourselves, your lusts, your relations, while the God of heaven is neglected! And the worship and service due unto Him alone is hereby idolatrously given to other things!

How are you doing? Are things clicking into place a bit? You may need a moment just to see what these diagnostic tools are revealing about your heart. Don't pass on too quickly if you have sensed something showing up on your mental radar for the first time. Take a moment to think about it.

## Two kinds of idols
Let's take it a stage further. We need another diagnostic tool, and this is one of the tools I have found most helpful. The idea is that there are different kinds of idols: deep idols and surface idols.[4]

### Surface idols
Surface idols are things like the car you do have or the husband you don't. Many of these are good things that we treat inappropriately, getting too concerned, preoccupied, proud or obsessed with them. It could mean doing the Scripture

reading in church or keeping your lawn nicely trimmed, securing a promotion at work or being complimented for having nicely behaved kids. Not all are good, however: they include pornography and gambling.

### Deep idols

Deep idols are the goals that lie behind the surface idols. They are what we hope the surface idols will give us. Here are some examples: security, significance, power, approval, comfort, control.[5] They are less tangible and visible: they lie underneath what we desire, but they are actually what we hope the surface idols will give us.

### The process

What happens is that we see a *surface* idol (whether a good thing like getting married or a bad one like looking at an internet porn site) and hanker after it and even pursue it (because we think it will bring us a *deep* idol – our goal). Arguably behind all these lies a final, ultimate deep idol: happiness – because we are hot-wired to do what we think will make us happy. We do what we want to do because we think it will make us happy.[6]

## In God's place

Now there is nothing wrong in itself about wanting security or approval or control. The problem is that we want them too much. We put them in God's place. And we don't seek them in God and his provision for us in Christ.

How does it work? Here is a list of beliefs that are deep idols in many people's hearts. Interestingly, the person who drew up the list isn't even a Christian – but he had unusual insight into patterns of thinking that mess up people's lives.

## *Irrational and self-defeating beliefs*

- *Being liked and loved.* I must always be loved and approved by the significant people in my life.
- *Being competent.* I must always, in all situations, demonstrate competence, and I must be both talented and competent in some important area of life.
- *Having one's own way.* I must have my way, and my plans must always work out.
- *Being hurt.* People who do anything wrong, especially those who harm me, are evil and should be blamed and punished.
- *Being danger-free.* If anything or any situation is dangerous in any way, I must not be anxious and upset about it. I should not have to face dangerous situations.
- *Being problemless.* Things should not go wrong in life, and if by chance they do, there should be quick and easy solutions.
- *Being a victim.* Other people and outside forces are responsible for any misery experience. No-one should ever take advantage of me.
- *Avoiding.* It is easier to avoid facing life's difficulties than to develop self-discipline; making demands of myself should not be necessary.
- *Tyranny of the past.* What I did in the past, and especially what happened to me in the past, determines how I act and feel today.
- *Passivity.* I can be happy by being passive, by being uncommitted, and by just enjoying myself.[7]

Does any of that sound familiar? As the author of the book says, 'I am sure that you could add to the list.' He has described a forest of 'idol thoughts'.

### For example

Let's take an example. John erupted with very negative emotions when his wife wouldn't make dinner one evening. 'It's your turn,' she said. He exploded. Why was that? His surface idol was food. He couldn't get it and, being thwarted, he was angry. But what lay beneath? Arguably a cluster of 'deep' idols. The most obvious is a comfort idol: wanting physical comfort, because it would make him happy. But there may be more. His wife wouldn't do what he wanted. So another deep idol was thwarted: an idol of control. He wanted to control his wife because he thought that would make him happy too. He felt his wife was denying him affection and showing she didn't love him: he had an idol of needing approval, affection and love. It is possible that there were other deep idols too.

## Idol chart

Here is a chart showing the difference between deep idols and surface idols. I should emphasize again that most of

| Surface idol | Possible deep idol(s) |
| --- | --- |
| New car | Reputation |
| First-class degree | Success, reputation |
| Unbelievably neat garden | Control |
| A boyfriend | Security, comfort |
| New clothes | Impressing others |
| Perfect attendance record at church | Idol of my religious performance |
| Exotic summer holidays | Pleasure, reputation |
| Well-behaved children | Parenting success, reputation |
| A good meal on the table, a tidy house and a smiling wife | Control, comfort |
| An expensive new kitchen | Comfort, reputation |

these surface idols are idols only because we make them idols. God has given them as actual or potential good gifts (1 Timothy 4:4–5). It's our fault for turning them into idols, not his.

## The shirt I wanted so much

In my first year of work at a large book-printing company called Hazel Watson and Viney in Aylesbury,[9] shirts with very long pointed collars were in fashion. Yes, it was a while ago! The local Next store in Aylesbury had one in the shop window. I used to re-route my walk home from work so I could go past it. I'd have a quick look and imagine myself in it. It was a bit more expensive than the amount I usually paid for shirts, but not excessive.

I desperately wanted it. The reason was not the shirt in itself. You see, there was a girl at church I rather liked. My housemate liked her best friend and I liked her. I began to think that if I bought the white Next shirt with the long pointed collar, she'd be impressed. I started to fantasize about buying it, wearing it to church and her seeing me and turning her head. I began to think about this improbable scenario more than I did about God.

After some weeks of agonizing, I checked my bank balance, marched to the shop and bought the white shirt with the long pointed collar for £14.99.[10] Next Sunday I wore it to church. *She* never noticed. At least she *showed* no sign of noticing. I felt extremely flat. The long points always stuck up slightly, looking stupid, and I came to hate that shirt.

## Working out *your* idols

How do we work out what our idols are? One way is to ask ourselves diagnostic questions. Tim Keller suggests this sentence completion exercise:[11]

I will feel happy and my life will have meaning if_____
_____.

    . . . I have power and influence over others
    . . . I am loved and respected by_____
    . . . I have *this* kind of quality of life
    . . . I look great
    . . . people are dependent on me and need me
    . . . there is someone there to keep me safe
    . . . I am completely free from obligations to or
        dependence on others
    . . . I am being recognized for my accomplishments
    . . . I have wealth and nice possessions
    . . . I keep the rules of my religion
    . . . I am totally independent of religion and morality
    . . . this one person is in my life
    . . . my children and / or parents are happy and happy
        with me
    . . . Mr or Miss Right is in love with me

How would you complete the sentence? Be honest now! Write it in pencil if you have to, so you can rub it out before anyone else reads the book.

Notice that these examples are a mixture of surface and deep idols. Some of them are quite general – 'if I have *this* kind of quality of life'. If that is your deep idol, you will almost certainly have a more concrete surface idol – like having a new kitchen every five years (and the most fashionable one at that, regardless of expense).

## Listen to your feelings

Then there is another diagnostic test: our feelings. A helpful way to detect idols is to analyse our emotions. Albert Ellis (who drew up the list of irrational and self-defeating beliefs quoted above) suggests that 'when these kinds of belief are violated in a person's life, he or she tends to see the experience as terrible, awful, catastrophic'.

Idols leave their mark on our feelings. Try following the emotional 'evidence trail' by examining your experiences of strong emotions, particularly negative ones. These can be powerful inner desires to have, to do, to prevent, to ensure, to remove or to achieve something. Idolatry also shows in excessive negative feelings of disappointment, fear, anger, anxiety or even hatred.

This was the key in the personal story I told right at the beginning of the book, when I nearly split up with Debbie back in the summer of 1988. To be sad at a relationship going wrong is perfectly normal, but my friend Ian's pastoral insight was to see that my excessively strong reaction indicated that she had become an idol.

### Wired to feel

Why are our feelings a good test? Because we are wired to respond emotionally to events. When it seems as though our goals are thwarted, we will tend to feel negatively. When we fail to reach (or think we will fail to reach) an idolatrous goal, we will tend to feel very negatively. It could be anger, sadness, disappointment, frustration or even boredom (feeling that nothing else will satisfy us).

### Excessive emotion

Think back to a time when you had a very strong reaction – a reaction that would have looked a little excessive to any objective observer. I think many of us parents would do well to analyse why we get so cross with our children on occasion. Is it *only* because we are so tired and vulnerable to explode?

Or it is possible that the reason why we fly off the handle is that we are idolizing our children, making their affection, obedience, achievement and general good behaviour into idols, surface idols that we hope will bring us comfort or reputation? I suspect a lot of excessive parental reactions can be best understood as idolatrous – and that's just in my life.

If excessive reactions are telling, what are yours telling you about your idols?

> Bridget loved her work as an account manager. The clients, the products, the colleagues – it was just the job she had hoped for. She had a great boss – always support-ing and praising her. One day she handed in her monthly report and he hardly glanced at it. Three days later, still no response. Normally he was full of positive words. Her mood dived. The work seemed to slow to a snail's pace. It didn't seem great any more. She started to consider moving on. Talking it through with a friend over a latte, Bridget wondered why it mattered so much to her to be praised by her boss: surely the work was good whether he recognized it or not? Why did she need praise so much?

**Just a note**

There can be a danger of introspection and excessive self-examination that takes our eyes off Jesus. It is important for those of us who have tendencies that way to ensure that our quest for self-understanding doesn't become another kind of self-centredness. We should pursue idols in our hearts when we see bad fruit in our lives (Luke 6:43–45).[12]

The following chapters look at specific idols like material-ism, sex and people. Before you go on to them you may like to note what you are learning about yourself:

I think my surface idols are _____.

I think my deep idols are _____.

## For discussion or personal reflection
Read Psalm 73.

1.  Look at verses 1–14. What is the writer's problem?
    What negative emotions are there here? What do they
    indicate? How can you identify with him?
2.  In verses 15–20, what helps him to recover? Why do you
    think the temple has this effect?
3.  In verses 21–22, how does he understand the emotional
    and spiritual effect of his distorted thinking previously?
    How can you identify with him?
4.  Read verses 23–26 again. What do you tend to 'desire'
    (v. 25) more than God himself?
5.  How many antidotes to your idolatry can you find here?

## 2. NEEDS OR PREFERENCES?

### When are shoes your idol?

Bowing down to images of cats and cows; logging on for an hour or three of internet pornography late at night; giving in to a compulsion to shoplift. Some of our idols are very obvious. But sometimes the dividing line is not so clear. That is particularly true when the idol is something that isn't wrong in itself. Like shoes. How can you tell when you are idolizing shoes and when you are simply enjoying them? We can't live in a world without possessions and pleasant experiences. Even the poorest people I know in Sierra Leone have both possessions and joys. When are God's gifts idols and when are they, well, gifts?

### Need or prefer?

There may be no easy dividing line, but there is a way of looking at this issue that I think is along the right lines. It involves distinguishing between *needs* and *preferences*.

#### On the buses

On the backs of the buses in Cambridge they advertise their 'Dayrider' or weekly bus tickets. The advertisements portray a series of fictional characters, each with a photograph and a few sentences of their supposed speech about what they are going to do on 'My day (or week) in the City'. Some are off to visit new babies in hospital, others are playing squash or heading off to work. But most are off shopping, drinking, dancing and hoping to go home with someone else to sleep together. Oddly enough, buying a bus pass seems to be a kind of passport to success in all these hopes.[1]

It sounds banal, but the little stories are extraordinarily revealing about the dreams and expectations people have. In one of these twenty-first-century parables of urban life, there is a picture of a young woman. Among the opportunities her Dayrider bus pass provides is some shopping, because she 'must, absolutely must, have new jeans'.

### Must have

The giveaway is the 'must'. When we use words like 'should', 'must' and 'have to' about anything except God and very basic human duties, idolatrous desires are very likely lurking behind them. I 'must' have a girlfriend. My date 'must' be there on time. I 'must' buy the latest Killers CD. We 'must' do Christmas the way we have always done it. I 'should' be promoted. We 'have to' have an expensive foreign holiday. She 'has to' smile at me when I come into work.

In turn these thoughts (which may be much stronger than we admit) generate their own unpleasant consequences: insensitivity to others, pushiness, selfishness accompanied by negative emotions: 'When you think in this rigid, [must-driven] way you will frequently feel anxious, depressed, self-hating, hostile, and self-pitying.'[2]

### Choosing to prefer

What can we do? We can start with our language. Rather than insisting in an absolute way that we *must* have this, or that something *mustn't* happen to us, we should learn to express our desires as preferences.

> Your preferences [would] start off with 'I would very much
> *like* or *prefer* to have success, approval, or comfort' and then
> end with the conclusion, '*But* I don't *have* to have it. I won't
> die without it. And I could be happy (though not as happy)
> without it.'[3]

The writer I have quoted, Albert Ellis, isn't a Christian. His
world-view and his writing are in many ways rather anti-
Christian. For instance, he is trying to help people avoid
depression rather than worship God. But he has hit the bullseye
in helping us define idolatry in a world where much of what
we idolize is good and even God-given.

### Needs and desires in marriage

Here's how it works in marriage. In a helpful book, Dave
Harvey asks, 'Is it wrong to desire the gentle caress of a
husband's hand or the kind words from a wife's tongue?' It's
a hard question, isn't it? If we say, 'Yes – it's wrong!' we sound
very self-controlled and even spiritual, but we don't seem very
real. But if we say, 'No – it's natural to want those things', are
we giving in to our inner selfishness? Dave Harvey answers
his own question clearly: 'Absolutely not.'

He then goes on to suggest a similar distinction to the one
we thought about above:

> But even things that are good for a marriage can be corrupted
> if they are defined as needs. The problem is not that we
> desire – desire is completely natural: it's that our desires
> become juiced with steroids. It is not wrong to desire
> appropriate things like respect or affection from our spouses.
> But it is very tempting to justify demands by thinking of them
> as needs and then to punish one another if those needs are
> not satisfied.[4]

### *'Must have' or 'would like'*

The distinction between preferences and needs is crucial to a happy marriage. It is also crucial to avoiding idolatry for anyone. The idol is the expensive meal out we *have* to have; the new CD we *need* so absolutely. Here's how it could work for a single person. If you are single but long to be married, is that longing based on idolatrous expectations? 'To adopt the frame of mind that you just have to be married . . . is to be a *Titanic* looking for an iceberg.'[5]

Think about yourself. Can you see where you have turned desires into demands? Think of moments when preferences have become deep needs. Have you turned something good into an idol? Why not tell God how sorry you are and ask him for help to make the future different.

The alternative to turning good things into idols is not to renounce them completely. At least, most of the time for most of us it isn't. The recovering alcoholic will need to stay off alcohol completely and it may be similar for others with deep-seated and really destructive idols. But Paul doesn't tell the Corinthians that the answer to idolizing sex is to give it up completely. He tells them to sort out their sex lives properly.

> Since there is so much immorality, each man should have[6] his own wife, and each woman her own husband.
> (1 Corinthians 7:2 NIV; see also vv. 8–9)

### *Regulated wealth*

In his first letter to Timothy, Paul warns rich people 'not . . . to put their hope in wealth . . . but to put their hope in God' (1 Timothy 6:17). So it is clear where their sense of security and future happiness comes from: Christ, not money. But he then adds, interestingly, 'who richly provides us with everything for our enjoyment'. It is as if he senses that some might overreact to the warning. Certainly that danger is on his mind, because earlier he warned them:

> Some . . . forbid people to marry and order them to abstain from certain foods, which God created to be received with thanksgiving by those who believe and who know the truth.
> (1 Timothy 4:3)

Then he reinforces what he has just said by virtually repeating it:

> For everything God created is good, and nothing is to be rejected if it is received with thanksgiving, because it is consecrated by the word of God and prayer.
> (1 Timothy 4:4–5)

This is not written to persuade people to give up enjoying the pleasures of life, but it is very different from an uncontrolled drive for selfish pleasure. These things have been declared 'good' and therefore set aside for God's purposes (that is the meaning of the word 'consecrated'). Notice how God-centred it is: good things are to be received with 'thanksgiving'.

### Thanks, Lord

Thanksgiving means that we don't take them for granted. Thanksgiving shows that we are not assuming we deserve or need or must have them. Thanksgiving means that we don't see them as our right. Thanksgiving implies that we hold the gifts with loose fingers, ready to give them up if needed. Thanksgiving means that it is God we worship, adore, depend on, find our security in, seek our comfort from, and put first.

G. K. Chesterton put it this way:

You say grace before meals.
All right.
But I say grace before the play and the opera,
And grace before the concert and pantomime,
And grace before I open a book,
And grace before sketching, painting,
Swimming, fencing, boxing, walking, playing, dancing;
And grace before I dip the pen into the ink.[7]

## For discussion or personal reflection
Read Matthew 6:16–34.

1. What does Jesus warn us about here?
2. How do verses 32–34 relate to the issues raised in this chapter?
3. What are the good and legitimate things you 'have to have'?
4. What will it take to turn these into 'preferences' or 'desires'?
5. Who actually defines what you *need*?
6. What are the things you think God 'must' give you? What does this say about your relationship with him?
7. What is the more biblical way?

## 3. MORE AND MORE AND MORE

Greed is arguably one of the most socially acceptable forms of idolatry today. Ivan Boesky, the Wall Street insider-dealing wizard, spoke at a Californian business school. He said, 'I think greed is healthy. You can be greedy and still feel good about yourself.' He was given a standing ovation. His favourite T-shirt had on it the slogan 'He who owns the most when he dies, wins'.

Boesky was the basis for the character of Gordon Gecko played by Michael Douglas in the 1986 film *Wall Street*. Gecko simplified Boesky's creed into three words: 'Greed is good.' He also coined the macho slogan 'Lunch is for wimps', but we won't get into that.

### Greed makes the world get richer

Boesky was the leading spokesman of a huge cultural movement in Britain and America in the 1980s in which greed was proclaimed as good. To some extent the blame for that can be placed on the shoulders of the political leaders. They may not have been greedy themselves. They may not have approved of conspicuous consumption. They may have promoted self-restraint and giving to charity. But that was not the legacy that their policies and influence left behind. The legacy was a moral legalization of greed. In many ways it was a moral disaster for our society. We learned to idolize money.

### Credit boom

That was twenty or more years ago. But arguably that cultural movement sowed the seeds for a further explosion of greedy idolatry from 2000 to 2007. The stupendous growth of the Chinese economy (and other emerging economies) provided huge quantities of cheap manufactured goods. The careful Chinese saved their profits in Western economies, providing cheap credit, which meant loans with low interest levels.

Financial institutions wanted to expand their profits for shareholders, so they lent money to people who would previously have been seen as unlikely to be able to keep up the repayments of loans. Clever financiers developed sophisticated ways of bundling this debt up and passing it on to other institutions.

### Credit crunch

But it wasn't clever. It was a fake. These apparently sophisticated 'financial instruments' disguised the poor quality of the debt. And in 2008 the whole house of cards came crashing down. It was a house that had been built on greed – the idols of money and possessions; the urge for more and more and more.

## The root of all evil?

The Bible does not see money and possessions in themselves as sinful. You may be surprised: didn't Paul write that 'money is the root of all evil'? No. He actually wrote, 'The love of money is a root of all kinds of evil' (1 Timothy 6:10). Money and possessions are not in themselves wrong. Having them in moderation isn't in itself wrong.

> For everything God created is good, and nothing is to be rejected if it is received with thanksgiving, because it is consecrated by the word of God and prayer.
>
> (1 Timothy 4:4–5)

### Loving you too much

The love of money is very different. It *is* the root of multiple kinds of evil. In another letter, Paul writes about the excessive love of money that puts it in God's rightful place.

> Put to death, therefore, whatever belongs to your earthly nature:
> . . . greed, which is idolatry.
> (Colossians 3:5)

Paul describes greed as worship of a false god. Many contemporary attitudes to possessions and money are just that.

> For the unbelieving world money takes on divine status. It is
> the god of this age, a god for which many people are willing to
> sacrifice their happiness, their children, their health, indeed their
> own lives. This kind of zeal for income borders on the irrational
> and we are hardly remiss in thinking of it as religion.[1]

### Greed is insatiable

It was said of a Texas oil billionaire that 'no matter how much money he had, he was always poor in his own mind'. Here's how the writer of Ecclesiastes put it:

> Again I saw something meaningless under the sun:
> There was a man all alone;
>     he had neither son nor brother.
> There was no end to his toil,
>     yet his eyes were not content with his wealth.
> 'For whom am I toiling,' he asked,
>     'and why am I depriving myself of enjoyment?'
> This too is meaningless –
>     a miserable business!
> (Ecclesiastes 4:7–8)

> Those who love money never have enough;
>> those who love wealth are never satisfied with their income.
>
> (Ecclesiastes 5:10)

It is not winning the lottery that drives most people, but the thought of 'a little bit more'. Surveys have shown that most people say they would be content if their income rose by 20%. Arguably much marketing is based on persuading people that what they need is just a bit more to be happy or respected or successful or comfortable. And they never get there. The marketing men are satisfied. Their victims are not.

## Money enslaves us

Read this description of some Christians:

> Their property held them in chains . . . chains which shackled their courage and choked their faith and hampered their judgement and throttled their souls . . . They think of themselves as owners, whereas it is they rather who are owned; enslaved as they are to their own property, they are not the master of their money but its slaves.[2]

Was the author writing about Russian oligarchs? Arab oil sheikhs? Footballers' WAGs? No. The author was the early Christian leader Cyprian, writing in 258 BC! But what he wrote is true today; perhaps even more true today.

## Well-paid slaves

A minister of a church in an affluent area talked with me about the pressures on his congregation. It was more in sadness than criticism that he described many of his highly successful professional members as 'well-paid slaves'. When I shared this with another group of Christians, one man said afterwards that it summed up his relationship to his work completely.

We create the idol, but in the end we serve what we worship. Slowly desire for money and possessions takes over, and we become their slave. We do what they demand rather than what God demands or common humanity demands. As Peter puts it, 'People are slaves to whatever has mastered them' (2 Peter 2:19).

> Money first enslaves people and then laughs at them as it fails to provide the happiness it promised.[3]

If you find that your better nature and your higher aspirations are being consistently put aside in favour of doing what will get you more money and possessions, you are worshipping money.

### Keeping money for ourselves

Evidence of idolizing money comes in our tendency to keep far too much of our income for ourselves. This is the classic miser profile brilliantly described by novelists – and none better than Charles Dickens's Ebenezer Scrooge in *A Christmas Carol*, who resented giving his staff a day off for Christmas and used to spend it doing his accounts.

Love of money makes people mean. We don't want to share it with others. We find all sorts of rationalizations and excuses. Sadly, rich people are often the most tight-fisted. Survey after survey shows that in so many countries poorer people give a higher percentage of their income to charity than rich people. Think about that for a moment: it is extraordinary. Rich people have far, far more than poorer people of what economists call 'disposable income'. Disposable income means the money you don't need simply to survive. It's where charitable giving comes from. And rich people keep more of it for themselves! Does that commend riches for their morally improving effect?

### Loving God with our money – not!

Earlier I said greed is when we love money more than God. That's true, but here's another thing to add to it. Greed is when we love money more than God and do not love God with our money. Refusing to share our money is a sign that we have made money our God.

### Feeling great through shopping

It isn't just the possessions that become idols. It's the shopping! In a profound piece of writing, Carl Trueman describes what all too often happens to us as we shop:

> When I buy something, then for a split second, I become god; I, Carl Trueman, use my divine powers to transubstantiate a worthless piece of paper or plastic into a loaf of bread, a book, a car, a house. This momentary self-deification satisfies my idolatry of self, but only for a moment; it has to be repeated again and again and again if I am to keep myself persuaded that I am indeed god, master of all I survey.[4]

As Carl shows, we seek a 'fix', a 'high', a 'hit' not so very unlike the escape from reality that drug abusers inject or inhale into their bloodstreams. For that moment, our anxieties melt away. As we right-click on our mouse and as the virtual button on our screens marked 'Place your order' magically depresses, the sense of power and peace floods through our souls.

Then, as the screen changes to one with the soothing words 'Your order has been accepted', there is a slight sense of emptiness, but we read on down and see that delivery is scheduled for only three days' time.

### The buzz from the buzzer

Each morning we wait expectantly for the postman. Eventually

the bell goes and there he is, our parcel in his hand. Eagerly
we take hold of it. If the purchase is supposed to be a secret
from our parents or wife or sensible housemate, we quickly
spirit it away to be opened in private. If there is no secret, we
just rip the bubble-wrap off it and find . . . what? A solution
to all our problems? A god in plastic form? The key to intellectual distinction? The secret to looking a million dollars?
Or just a CD. A book. A skirt.

### That empty feeling again

Shopping, in which we invest so much time, energy and hope,
often leaves us with an odd empty feeling. Not just disappointment: the new car may well get us from A to B; the football
can be kicked around satisfactorily enough. But the sense of
total control, meaning and security we had hoped would last
just ebbs away. We are left exactly where we were – but with
our bank account a few pounds lighter. We have the same
need and so the cycle begins again.

### Idols of luxury

Idolizing things can take the form of a desire for luxury goods.
Every now and then my Saturday newspaper comes with a
free insert called simply *Lux: The Best of Everything*. The most
recent one features such necessities as a pair of tortoiseshell
sunglasses for the 'sophisticated sunbather' at £625. I know a
church-planter in Sierra Leone who could have a pile of mud
bricks and a small plot of land turned into a house for less
than that.

Other must-have items include a Swiss watch for £12,910
(not a possession, the advertisement assures us, but 'a legacy
for the next generation' – what self-serving drivel!), a cashmere
sweater for £510, and then, for those jaded by all that tedious
shopping, there is the Ultimate Thrill adventure holiday in

Southern Africa which will get the adrenalin flowing in the veins again through driving A1 race cars, flying a decommissioned Harrier Jump Jet, racing a monohull yacht and diving with great white sharks, not to speak of quad-bikes, sleeping in the desert, meeting penguins and tracking with bushmen, all in eleven days (honestly – it's all in eleven days), and all for a cool £12,260 (for two).

I have to admit, I normally throw *Lux* away unread.[5] It's not that I am really tempted by its contents, nor that I am jealous of those who can afford them. It's that reading it tends to lower my guard against the inner tiger of my own longing for more. For me it's not fast cars or luxury accessories, but books and CDs. I am pathetically vulnerable to thinking that yet another book will finally make me well read, able to hold my head up high in the university city where I live.

### I got 25% off!

Another kind of 'thing idolatry' is the lure of the bargain. People who would never dream of saying they needed a new pair of shoes when they were at full price suddenly develop an irresistible and unarguable need for them when there is 25% off. This is one of the ways in which modern marketing penetrates all our defences, persuading us that we should open our wallets because it is a good deal. We feel doubly good: we have something new and we have saved money. We triumphantly proclaim to our housemates how much we have saved. We conveniently ignore the fact that we didn't really need it and therefore we have lost money instead. I know. I've been down that track too many times.

What is your area of vulnerability? Shoes? Shirts? CDs? Holidays? Cars? Is the area to watch the internet? When the new La Redoute catalogue thumps onto your doorstep? A trip to IKEA? The January sales? Remember: the idea that more and more will make us happy is simply wrong. More and more will just make us want more and more.

## Escaping from greed
Here are some pointers to turning from the idol of greed.

### Grow in generosity
The answer to greed is not just self-restraint. Nor is it to try to do without money. It is to enjoy what God gives and to develop a generous spirit. Rich Christians have a special responsibility to do this. And almost everyone reading this book is rich in world terms. Paul has important words for rich Christians:

> Command those who are rich in this present world . . . to do
> good, to be rich in good deeds, and to be generous and willing
> to share. In this way they will lay up treasure for themselves as
> a firm foundation for the coming age, so that they may take hold
> of the life that is truly life.
> (1 Timothy 6:17–19)

C. S. Lewis has some challenging words that ought to get under our skin:

> I do not believe one can settle how much we ought to give. I am
> afraid the only safe rule is to give more than we can spare. In
> other words, if our expenditure on comforts, luxuries,
> amusements, etc., is up to the standard common among those
> with the same income as our own, we are probably giving away
> too little. If our charities do not at all pinch or hamper us, I
> should say they are too small. There ought to be things we should
> like to do and cannot do because our charitable expenditure
> excludes them.[6]

But that is not enough. We need something to release us from our greed and free us to be generous. We need contentment.

### Learn contentment

> Godliness with contentment is great gain.
> (1 Timothy 6:6)

Nothing is more important in battling greed than to be content – and the weed of greed cannot grow in the soul soil of contentment.

An older writer suggests that:

> A godly heart enjoys much of God in everything he has and knows how to make up all wants in God himself.[7]

Someone put this idea into a moving prayer:

> All the good things of life are less than nothing when compared with his love, and with one glimpse of thy electing favour.
> All the treasurers of a million worlds could not make me richer, happier, more contented for his unsearchable riches are mine.[8]

See how much God has promised us:

> Keep your lives free from the love of money and be content with what you have, because God has said,
>> 'Never will I leave you;
>>> never will I forsake you.'
> So we say with confidence,
>> 'The Lord is my helper; I will not be afraid.
>>> What can human beings do to me?'
> (Hebrews 13:5–6)

But that kind of contentment is not automatic. I love the realism of this writer:

> I believe that it is possible with God's help to be content whatever state we are in. But such contentment is often attained only after a long spiritual struggle.[9]

Contentment isn't instant. You can't go to your pastor for an injection. It can't be ordered from Amazon. It is learned slowly and over years, not delivered by the postman next day. We think we have got it and then we lurch back into retail therapy or worry. We make it through an overdraft crisis or we resist the temptation to go for broke with our new car. We get a bonus and give more than 10% of it to the church or a Christian worker. Then we slip backwards with something we didn't really need – that swish skirt from TK Maxx.

### Making progress

But all the time the direction is upward. The Holy Spirit is at work. He is leading us on and we find ourselves trusting God more and worshipping money less. And we find ourselves being more content. Or we should be: unless we are content we will never stop being affected by greed.

### You are secure!

The heart of contentment is security in God. The author to the Hebrews doesn't simply say, 'Be content', as if an anxious person could turn off their anxiety like a switch. He says we can be content because God is totally, irrevocably committed to us. 'You need security? You got security!' Christians have security in God. He has said he'll never leave you. When you hear that promise you can say, 'OK, God is going to help me: I don't have to be afraid! What can anyone do to take God away? Nothing.' In Paul's words, we 'put our hope in God', not in our money. And we find freedom.

I have had pensions with Robert Maxwell, perhaps the biggest crook in British business history, and with the Equitable Life, which found itself badly overextended by rash promises to certain investors. Both minor crises were steps forward in Christ's constant training programme about the uncertainty of earthly riches and the total security of placing my needs in God's hands.

### Leave it with him

Take those financial insecurities to God and leave them with him. If you feel financially insecure, this speaks to your heart more directly. Be sure that God is your Father. He knows your needs.

Forget your fantasies of winning the lottery or having just that little bit more. Turn your longings instead onto Almighty God. Set your heart on him. Remember that he is strong. Remember that he is loving. Put your trust in your heavenly Father.

As one student who was baptized at my church said in his testimony: 'I have found it so hard to trust him when things are difficult, but the more I have trusted in him, the more he has guided and looked after me. Through this I have come to realize that God really is sovereign over all things, and I am so thankful he offers something so much greater than any of my worries on this earth.'[10]

### Simply happy

Another way to grow in contentment is to decide to embrace simplicity.[11] My mother is the person who has most modelled this for me. She and my father grew up in the Second World War at a time when things were rationed by law. The government allocated you coupons for sweets, clothes and all sorts of basic foods. Without the coupons you couldn't buy the items. People learned to get by with less, to patch clothes.

Rationing stopped a few years after the war ended. My sister and I used to joke that it continued for decades in our house. But I think we appreciated my parents' attempt to live a bit more simply than perhaps their income would have allowed and to realize that happiness didn't lie in constant acquisition.

### Less is more

Almost all of us think that living more simply would make us less happy. If we have God, we are wrong. The need to reduce our carbon footprint is bringing back all sorts of rather old-fashioned ideas like recycling, mending, passing on children's clothes and decluttering our lives.

How could you simplify your life? What would hold you back? Why would it be worth it?

## For discussion or personal reflection

Read 1 Timothy 6:6–10, 17–19.

1. Summarize Paul's view of money and possessions, trying to get his balance right. Which way are you unbalanced in your heart attitude to them?
2. What is the connection between 'godliness' and 'contentment'? Why do we end up with the opposite so often?
3. What are the dangers of money and possessions to the Christian's well-being? How does this play out in your own life?
4. What stops us being 'rich in good deeds' and 'generous' (v. 18)?

## 4. LUST

Posters had gone up all round college. A student debating society was starting up. The first debate was designed to draw the punters in: the motion was 'This house believes that sex belongs in marriage'. The organizers asked me to propose it. Like a mug, I agreed.

On the evening, I stood up and looked around the room: I couldn't see more than two people who would agree with me out of three or four dozen. I felt as though it was more like a darts match than a debate, with me as the dartboard. Mouthing a silent prayer, I began my speech by reading a passage from Proverbs.

> Should your springs overflow in the streets,
> > your streams of water in the public squares?
> Let them be yours alone,
> > never to be shared with strangers.
> May your fountain be blessed,
> > and may you rejoice in the wife of your youth.
> (Proverbs 5:16–18)

As the passage unfolded, some of the audience sniggered because they thought they had detected an unintentional innuendo. I picked up on the laughter, but remarked gently that the innuendo was entirely intentional. The images of fountains *were* sexual, but the text used them entirely approvingly as part of a portrayal of marital sex. They fell quiet, amazed perhaps that the Bible could be positive about sex in that rapturous way.

Astonishingly, we won the debate. I am not sure it changed anyone's behaviour. In fact, I rather doubt it. But for a few moments I had been able to portray a positive alternative to the casual sleeping around that was so prevalent.

You may wonder why I have started a chapter on lust in this way. The reason is that so often Christian teaching on sex has been too negative. Augustine, a great church leader in the fourth century AD, for instance, thought that sex was only acceptable as a way of producing children. Any sexual pleasure, even between man and wife, was automatically wrong. The Bible, by contrast, celebrates sexual love within marriage as a great gift from God.

So we must not make the mistake of thinking that having sexual desires and being sexual beings is wrong and sinful. Sexuality is God's gift to us. But it is a broken gift: like every-thing in this world, it was affected by the fall. Perhaps more than any other part of us.[1]

## Celebrated in song
Sexual pleasure is celebrated in song both in the Bible and in all kinds of literature, as one of the most intense we can experience. The urge to have children, the longing for deep and unique intimacy and our appetite for the sheer physical exhilaration of sex all mean that our sexual drives are among the most powerful God has given. So it is not surprising that sexuality becomes an idol for many people, a different god to worship, what the Bible calls 'lust':

> For of this you can be sure: no immoral, impure or greedy
> person – such a person is an idolater – has any inheritance in
> the kingdom of Christ and of God.
> (Ephesians 5:5)

Paul says here that there are patterns of sin that shut people out of God's eternal family. Immorality, impurity and greed bar us from heaven. He sums up the greedy person as 'an idolater'.[2] The passage as a whole is about sexual sin, so it seems reasonable to interpret 'greedy' here as indicating 'unrestrained sexual greed'. For, 'Along with greed for riches and power, sexual lust is an idolatrous obsession; it places self-gratification or another person at the centre of one's existence, rather than the Creator.'[3]

## Heavenly sex
Sexual idolatry is as prone to enslave us as any of the other kinds of idols. Our drives are so strong that it is too easy to assume they are pushing us towards something of ultimate significance that deserves our worship. In the centuries when the Bible was written there was often sacred prostitution in the idol temples. In our day, sex is similarly deified.

> Lust is so unhealthy because it can captivate a whole person and monopolize his or her energies to the exclusion of everything unrelated to that passion. To lust is to be in the service of an idol.[4]

Lust is uncontrolled sexual desire. It can be expressed in actual physical actions or in our inner thought world. It makes sex into an idol that brings us comfort and perhaps even power. 'Isn't that a potent idol of our time? We live in a sex-orientated society where an individual is encouraged to see their very identity in terms of their sex-lives.'[5]

## Blitzed by sex
That encouragement comes in so many forms. One friend told me she (yes, *she!*) had received over one hundred emails in a single week offering her Viagra over the internet.

Computer pop-ups offer instant release from boredom at the click of a mouse. Supposedly serious newspapers sell themselves with banners along the top of the front page containing the word 'sex'.[6] Why? Because sex sells.

Virtually all portrayal of sex on television sells us a story of instant total gratification as the norm on a first date. Scriptwriters conveniently ignore the realities of sexual adjustment that can take months or years – and the frequently painful consequences of one-night stands and affairs.[7] Christian teenagers meet with bafflement or opposition in school PHSE[8] lessons when they try to argue that sex before marriage is harmful. Outside school their friends boast of their experiences and express amazement that they are still virgins.

## Just a little treat?

These invitations to sexual immorality find receptive ground in our hearts. You read the TV schedule. A voice whispers, 'It's been a hard week – feast your eyes on this piece of naked flesh and let the pain float away.' The drama or soap opera whose characters swap beds like boys swapping football cards broadcasts a hidden message: 'Go a bit further with your boyfriend – it feels good so it must be right. Everyone's doing

> Josh reckoned that he and Hannah had a pretty good sex life. Over ten years of marriage they had adjusted fairly well to each other and knew how to give each other pleasure. One night Josh suggested sex. Hannah made a face and said she was tired. Josh flew into a rage and slept in the spare bedroom. Next morning he was rather shaken by the fury of his reaction – but unsure what he could do next.

it – you owe it to yourself to have this intimacy.' Paul calls
these messages 'empty words' (Ephesians 5:6).[9] And they
are. They are words that seem to promise bliss, but deliver
emptiness.

## Dethroning the idol of sex

First we must repent: this means recognizing that our lust is
wrong, that it is insulting God by pushing him off the throne
of our hearts and putting sex there instead. Then we must
seek forgiveness. There is no sexual lust so powerful or embar-
rassing that it cannot be forgiven. Jesus' death is a sufficient
payment for all our sins, sexual sins too.

Then we need to adopt a series of measures to deal with
our lustful idolatry. Again we see that the alternative to a sin
is not just self-control, but love.

### Purity and the promises of God

The first step is to remember all God has given us.

> Since we have these promises, dear friends, let us purify ourselves
> from everything that contaminates body and spirit, perfecting
> holiness out of reverence for God.
> (2 Corinthians 7:1)

The purity comes from trusting the promises. Not just from
resolutions, accountability, realizing that sexual impurity is
wrong, or anything else: it comes from realizing who we are,
realizing who God is, and choosing to focus on the amazing
love of God that he has promised to us. The way to escape
impurity is to remember God's promise to live with us and be
our God and for us to be his people; to remember his call to
holiness and his promise to 'receive us' and to be our Father
and to make us his sons and daughters.

### My body: whose temple?

As you fight sexual idolatry, realize your body is a temple for the worship of God, not a pagan temple for idol worship. Then realize that your boyfriend's or girlfriend's body is also a temple for the worship of God. His temple is not one for you to worship your sex idol on. 'His temple, not your playground!'[10]

### Love not lust

Why is it that someone visits a pornographic website? Is it simply out of curiosity? Sometimes maybe. Much more often it is because of a deep sense of personal pain or worthlessness. A feeling of loneliness and need. It is an attempt to find something to dull the pain. Almost every kind of compulsive behaviour is an attempt to anaesthetize a deep personal pain. Unless you reach the core of that pain you won't really deal with the behaviour. So if you want to deal with lust, don't think the love of God is irrelevant. It is right at the heart of what you need.

Paul says that we are 'dearly loved children . . . Christ loved us and gave himself up for us' (Ephesians 5:1–2). What we need is not less love, but more. We need to realize that God's love is sufficient for us; that it is infinitely better to gaze on the beauty and glory of Almighty God than on pictures of men or women to whom we are not married.

### Learn to love people, not lust for objects

Each time we nurse sexual fantasies about someone we are treating them like an object for our gratification and literally dehumanizing them. Instead we need to learn to love them with the self-giving love Christ has for us. Instead we need to work out ways of serving other people in self-giving love.

Jane used to spend a lot of time enjoying romantic fantasies. In her mind she'd drift away to thoughts of weddings and honeymoons with moonlit beaches. Sometimes she'd imagine walking down the aisle with men she knew, even though some of them were already married. She argued that it was just a bit of pretend, a way of coping with the loneliness she felt. The pastoral worker at her church took her out for coffee and asked her what she spent most of her time thinking about. Jane turned red, but was honest. She agreed with the pastoral worker that it wasn't a great way to honour God: when she threw herself into her house group with renewed energy, she felt much better.

### Win the battle of the mind

Paul reminds us that we were taught to be made new in the attitude of our minds (see Ephesians 4:23). As with all idol wars, the battle is won and lost in the mind.

By the mind, I don't just mean your rational thoughts (knowing that sex outside marriage is sin), but also your mental images (that girl or boy you mentally undress) and associations (the sight of someone else's nakedness means a distraction from my pain; fantasy or orgasm will make me happy).

We are in a culture that is sexually explicit and immoral at the same time. Advertising executives know that sex sells. Clothing designers try to produce designs that are more than flattering, they are deliberately enticing. We are bombarded with lies about sex from Hollywood.

### The truth will set you free

So it is all the more important that we are convinced of the truth about sex and then live it out in our mind. We should develop mental disciplines. For this we may need to do more than just repeat to ourselves that sexual sin is wrong. We need to recapture our imaginations.

### Battling with internet porn

One of the most common ways people worship sex as a god these days is through the internet. Two students who were baptized in our church within a few weeks of each other both explained how internet porn had got a grip on them.[11] Here is one of them: 'In my second year at Cambridge . . . I was a little depressed. I was lonely and striving for something. The internet became my friend and I wasted my time on impure material. Much of society does not help. Take the *Sun* newspaper: on one page they have a page 3 girl and on the next they have a story about a sex pervert – but I made these decisions and was wallowing in a vicious cycle of sin.'

Many Christians become hooked on internet porn. As with all addictions, it starts with a few trials and becomes a habit and then an addiction. Furtive hours are spent looking at images that do not really satisfy. Chatrooms give an illusion of intimacy and the thrill of the forbidden, but leave us empty and diminished.

### Only Jesus

Here is the story of Simon (not his real name), a friend of mine who explains how the Lord helped him shake off his internet porn compulsions.

> However much I tried it, the will-power of 'just don't look at it' never worked for me. I could go for a few days, and then the hole left just had to be filled. But then God made me realize that my choice was not simply between looking at porn and not. It was between desiring Jesus, who would satisfy, or desiring something

else, which wouldn't. The struggle didn't become easy then, but it
did become winnable, because I realized I had to choose not just
to walk away from something, but to walk towards someone.[12]

## Different images

Another friend, a bit older than Simon, shared with me how he
fought mental obsessions with women to whom he wasn't
married. He would notice a girl, feel a sense of attraction, and
then let it turn into mental fantasy. He told me that to fight it,
he would play a different videotape in his mind. Not the precious
episodes of amazing sex and high romance with the lady in
question, but the next episode, the one that followed his wife
finding out. He would picture her anger and tears, the look of
accusation and disappointment in her face. He would make
himself watch the scene as he left the family home, his children
crying, his youngest daughter clinging to his legs, begging him
not to go, failing to understand, his older sons looking scorn-
fully at their father, hating his hypocrisy and betrayal of them
all. He found it a pretty powerful antidote to his fantasies.

Jane had another mental strategy. She developed a powerful
sense of attraction to a close friend of her husband. She fought
it, but it wouldn't shift. His face kept coming to mind, accompanied with romantic visions and even sometimes sexual
arousal. She prayed about it and asked God to help. She felt
the Holy Spirit giving her a different image: of a waterfall.
When the man's face or body came into her mind she would
instantly switch to this picture of the waterfall, of cascading
pure white water. She would keep it there for as long as it took
for the temptation of lust to pass.

## What about you?

Are you worshipping sex, as an idea or physical reality, inside
or outside marriage? Do you invest in sex your hopes for

ultimate experience? Do you trust in sexual pleasure as your greatest comfort, rather than God? Are you serving the sex god, with all those hours on the internet? Has the idol of sex enslaved you? Repent and do something better: find your deepest satisfaction in love.[13]

One young man in a gay relationship found freedom in some words from Jeremiah: 'For I know the plans I have for you . . . plans to prosper you and not to harm you, plans to give you hope and a future' (29:11).

> It was with those words that I was powerfully cut to the heart and brought to faith in Jesus Christ, graciously rescued by God out of a long term gay relationship. Aged 24 my life was turned upside down and completely revolutionised by the amazing love of God which quite literally drove out the idolatrous love I had developed for my partner.[14]

## For discussion or personal reflection
Read Ephesians 5:1–10.

1. What in this passage speaks to your sexual identity and practice?
2. How has your sexuality, straight or gay, married or single, become an idol to you? Are there big choices you need to make? Is there idolatrous love or sexual compulsion which is ruining your walk with God?
3. How do verses 1–2 help you break free?

## 5. BEAUTY AND BODY IMAGE

### The incredible doll

Every second, two Barbie dolls are purchased somewhere in the world. I wonder if those buying them realize just how totally unrealistic they are. Barbie's proportions in a live human being would produce a woman over 7 feet tall with a 44-inch bust, a 17-inch waist and 40-inch hips. Yet that is the shape of the dolls girls play with. No wonder many women have a deep sense of dissatisfaction with their bodies.

#### *Complaining to the manufacturer*

In her great book *Wanting To Be Her: Body Image Secrets Victoria Won't Tell You*, Michelle Graham has this imaginary dialogue with God:

| | |
|---|---|
| God: | Do you know that I made everything you see? |
| Michelle: | Oh yes Lord and what a great job you did! Down to every last detail – bravo! Standing ovation even! |
| God: | Do you know that I made you too? |
| Michelle: | Right. Good job. The human body is pretty amazing. And so is mine, well all except for my hair. It's a little limp and the colour needs some livening up. |
| | Oh and my thighs don't exactly look swimsuit ready. And now I think about it you could have |

improved slightly on my chest. It's not like
everybody else's. Oh and my skin's too freckly,
and there's the matter of my height, and my hips
and my eyes.

Actually God, I have a short performance
review I've typed up for you that might help in
your future people making. I mean really great job
in general with humanity. But my particular body
could have used a better design.[1]

### Men too

Michelle says what many people feel about their bodies. Nor
is this simply a female problem. According to the British
Department of Health, between 2003/4 and 2005/6 the UK
saw a massive 90% increase in the number of men reported
with eating disorders, whereas in the same period the increase
in cases reported amongst women was 25%. Eating disorders
have deep roots in all sorts of personal experiences and needs,
but one way they express themselves is through comparing
our bodies unfavourably with others.

### It's Liz!

In 2008, *New Woman* magazine[2] polled 5,000 women to find
the 'British Body Idol'. Yes, they used the word 'idol'. The
result was Liz Hurley, who is apparently the perfect blend of
curves, grooming and toning. But maintaining that figure is
hard work. She once confessed to eating just one full meal a
day and snacking on six raisins. Watercress soup is a staple of
her diet.

The editor of *New Woman* commented, 'For most of us, a
body like Elizabeth Hurley's would require a lifetime of
sacrifice.' So if you want to look good – really good – be
prepared for a lot of watercress soup. And then see if it makes

you really happy. That sounds like a pretty extreme kind of idolatry to me.

### Bodies on altars

Oddly enough, a lifetime of sacrifice of our bodies is precisely what the Bible calls for too. But it is sacrifice of a rather different kind. This sacrifice is far healthier – physically, emotionally and spiritually. And it will make us far happier than daily watercress soup. Even if you like it.

> Therefore, I urge you, brothers [and sisters], in view of God's mercy, to offer your bodies as living sacrifices, holy and pleasing to God – this is your spiritual act of worship.
> (Romans 12:1 NIV)

I must have read that a hundred times before I realized the implications of this text for the way we see our bodies and our physical appearance. God says, 'I want you to please me with your body. I want you to give *me* pleasure with it.' Isn't that what the text says?

Paul reminds us of 'the mercies of God'. Jesus cared enough about your body to die to redeem it. God wanted your body so much that he suffered in a body to make it his.

> 'He himself bore our sins' in his body on the cross, so that we might die to sins and live for righteousness.
> (1 Peter 2:24)

When we become Christians we don't leave our bodies and go to heaven. God calls us to serve him on earth in our bodies. Our bodies are not just for us to do what we want with. Our bodies are not to please other people, or even ourselves. They are to please God.

## Spring-cleaned minds

To please God with our bodies, our minds need renewing:

> Do not conform to the pattern of this world, but be transformed
> by the renewing of your mind.
> (Romans 12:2)

An effectively consecrated body needs *a changed mindset*. To
make our bodies pleasing to God, we need to have our thinking
transformed. There are two stages: what we change from and
what we change to.

### The beauty myth

What is the pattern of the world in regard to body image and
beauty? What is the mould of thinking we need to break? The
culturally dominant pattern of thinking in the Western world
has been named 'the beauty myth' by Naomi Wolf, in her
powerful book of that title.

She argues that we live in a cultural situation with regard
to physical appearance which is entirely new historically. The
reason is technology, starting in the nineteenth century with
photography and massed printed media and now extending
to moving images on film and TV. The result is that every day
most of us are bombarded with images of other people's faces
and bodies. It is a hugely influential part of what Paul calls
'the pattern of the world'. If we are going to stop the world
squeezing us into its mould, we need to understand what that
mould is. If we are going to stop being conformed to it, we
need to prick the bubble.

### The myth: subjective and narrow definitions of beauty

God loves variety. That's why we are all so different. There
is huge variety in creation. But commercial interests prefer

to standardize. So they can make money by exploiting the insecurities of the majority who don't fit the ideal pattern. Which they define and choose. And change when it suits them. So they decree that certain sizes and shapes are OK – while others are not.

Wolf refers to 'the myth of the official breast'. She writes about 'official breast propaganda' which 'make[s] virtually any woman feel that her breasts alone are too soft or low or sagging or small or big or weird or wrong'.[3]

It applies to other parts of the body too. One analyst reckoned that only 3% of white women had the underlying bone structure required to meet the standards of facial beauty as defined by the fashion industry.

### The beauty myth: literally an illusion

The movie *Pretty Woman* was advertised with a poster which showed Julia Roberts and Richard Gere standing back to back. Except that it wasn't Julia Roberts. Well, not her body anyway. It was deemed substandard, so a photo of her head was pasted onto a photograph of an anonymous model with better proportions or whatever. Julia Roberts wasn't good enough!

> In reality the mass beauty ideal is unrealistic and unattainable in real life except by extraordinary means – even by the models and actresses themselves.[4]

In a remarkable interview, actress and film star Julianne Moore recalled sitting around with an unnamed actress friend who was looking at a glossy magazine. '"Why don't I look like that?" exclaimed the friend. Then she looked more closely. It *was* her. After the make-up people had done their stuff, and the lighting man had weaved his magic, and perhaps above all when the photo had been brushed up with the latest software. The image wasn't real.'[5]

We have been sold a lie.

### The beauty myth: false promises
The modern beauty myth is an idol which seems to offer us control of our lives, but in fact takes control of our hearts.

> Media images work in us like a power. In their role as idols, they fill the space of the rejected Creator in which we try to anchor our rootless selves. Idols are agents of control. As self-created false gods they provide order in the midst of cultural chaos. They tell us how to live and who we are. What the idol promises is an illusion of power over our life, an illusory agency to become what we wish, and a fraudulent identity from which to speak.[6]

The idol whispers its lies:

- If you're thin, you'll be happy.
- If you had a 36-inch bust, you'd feel OK.
- If you got a six-pack like David Beckham, you'd be a real man.

### Exploited!
But idols don't make us happy. They can't – they aren't God. And they aren't designed to make us happy.

> Magazines must project the attitude that looking one's age is bad because hundreds of millions of dollars in advertising revenue comes from people who would go out of business if age looked good . . . The advertisers depend on making women feel bad enough about their faces and bodies to spend more money on them than they would if they felt beautiful.[7]

This is the honest admission of a woman who reads a lot of women's magazines:

> I buy them as a form of self-abuse. They give me a weird mixture of anticipation and dread, a sort of stirred up euphoria. Yes! Wow! I can be better starting from right this moment. Look at her! Look at *her*! But right afterward, I feel like throwing out all my clothes and everything in my refrigerator and telling my boyfriend never to call me again and blowtorching my whole life. I'm ashamed to admit that I read them every month.[8]

That's what idolizing beauty does to us: it offers hope, but it delivers self-hatred and enslavement.

## No-one's happy

The beauty myth seems to promise good health: if you are incredibly thin and very tanned, you'll be healthy. But:

> [I]n a survey of 33, 000 women 75% of those aged 18–35 believed they were fat, while only 25% were medically overweight; 45% of the underweight women thought they were too fat.[9]

## Beauty and the knife

Cosmetic surgery has exploded in popularity in the USA, and the UK is rapidly following the American path. Tummy tucks, face lifts, breast enhancements, Botox injections, liposuction to extract the fat we've accumulated round our waists or hips – they are all sold as the way to feeling great again.

> Small breasts or breasts that have decreased in size following childbirth and breast feeding can be a source of concern or embarrassment to a woman. But breast enlargement surgery is one way to make you feel more confident and feminine again.[10]

Here are two of the reasons for breast enlargement offered by one Harley Street clinic:

- To improve self-esteem and self-image.
- To help create a more proportionate figure and hence make clothes buying much more enjoyable.[11]

The five most popular procedures for men at one clinic are nose reshaping, chest reduction, liposuction, ear reshaping and face/neck lift. Here are two of the 'facts' offered as reasons for having the last of these procedures:

- The desire for men to stay young looking is more and more important nowadays.
- Face lift and neck lift are amongst the most efficient cosmetic surgery procedures to fight against the sign of ageing.[12]

I want to ask, 'Why? Who says?'

### More and more surgery

Professionals involved in cosmetic surgery report clients returning again and again for more. Breast enlargements don't overcome the underlying insecurity, so repeated injections of Botox are needed. Face lifts are followed by neck lifts which are followed by nose jobs and chemical skin peels. Liposuction can remove fat but can't deal with comfort eating issues, so further procedures are needed. There may be some people (with, say, uncomfortably large breasts, or a nose left distorted after an accident) for whom this kind of elective cosmetic surgery is sensible, but most are victims of the beauty myth and those who exploit our insecurities financially.

We're looking for security and happiness in the wrong place. We need reprogramming. The beauty myth is a cruel, exploitative illusion. It's not real. Let's please God by rejecting it. We need to be renewed in our thinking about our bodies and our appearance.

## A new way of looking at those grey hairs

We spend millions on dyes to hide the effects of ageing. The Bible sees greying a little differently:

> Grey hair is a crown of splendour;
>     it is attained by a righteous life.
> (Proverbs 16:31 NIV)

Naomi Wolf contrasts two ways of looking at female ageing in particular:

> You could see the signs of female ageing as diseased, especially if you had a vested interest in making women too see them your way. Or you could see that if a woman is healthy she lives to grow old; as she thrives she reacts and speaks and shows emotion and grows into her face.
>
> Lines trace her thought and radiate from the corners of her eyes after decades of laughter closing together like fans as she smiles. When gray and white reflect in her hair, you could call it a dirty secret or you could call it silver or moonlight.
>
> Her body fills into itself, growing generous with the rest of her. The darkening under her eyes, the weight of their lids, their minute cross-hatching reveal that what she has been has left in her its complexity and richness.
>
> The maturing of a woman who has continued to grow is a beautiful thing to behold. Or if your ad revenue or your seven figure salary depend on it, it is an operable condition.[13]

Which way are you going to view it? I am not saying that we should never dye our hair (though if I ever did, I hate to think what my mother would say). That is a matter of personal choice. But the choice shouldn't be made because we think that grey or white hair is somehow less beautiful, or that ageing destroys beauty.

## Rewiring our minds means looking at Jesus

Religious art tends to show Jesus in a highly idealized way: blow-dried wavy hair, perfect features, a placid expression. Jesus wasn't, apparently, all that special to look at:

> He had no beauty or majesty to attract us to him,
>> nothing in his appearance that we should desire him.
> (Isaiah 53:2)

The implication is that people looked at Jesus and didn't see anything special. He didn't naturally stand out from the crowd. No-one would have used Jesus as a model, or put him on the front of a magazine for his looks. Just think about that for a moment: his face was physically nothing out of the ordinary. If he was like that and was also the most contented human being who has ever lived, doesn't that say something to us?

### The beauty of the cross

And yet the face of Jesus Christ is intensely beautiful for those with eyes to see its beauty – a beauty seen most on the cross.

The cross is where we find our security and our identity and our joy. The cross is where the burdens drop off our backs. The cross is where we find acceptance and forgiveness. The cross is where we find freedom from the compulsive need to please others. It's where we find the freedom to please God instead.

One Christian woman has really seen this profoundly:

> The cross is an unlikely location to find beauty. But as we turn
> and fix our eyes on Jesus, we look away from the false cultural
> idols, breaking their power. What cultural and media images have
> destroyed in our imagination the cross can restore. The son of
> God becoming sin for me restores [my vision] so that I can see
> what is truly beautiful.
>
> This renewal of the imagination has the power to release
> us from the constant pressure to compare ourselves to the false
> image. It allows us to look in the mirror without shame. We
> will see beauty where we saw lack. We will see our naked faces
> reflecting the love of God.[14]

### Accepting our bodies
Buried in his great hymn to marriage in Ephesians 5, Paul has
this common-sense observation:

> After all, people have never hated their own bodies, but they feed
> and care for them.
> (Ephesians 5:29)

Don't hate your body. Receive it. It's his gift to you. Are you
really going to say that he's made a mistake with you? Love
it. Feed it. Care for it for him. Please him with it.

Have you ever thanked God for your body? What, never?
Surely it is one of his greatest gifts to you. No body – no life!
Why not stop right now and simply say, 'Thank you, Lord, for
this body you've given me.'

### Caring for our bodies
Survival is one of our most basic instincts. God put it there.
It's programmed into us to care for ourselves. But in our age

of over-eating, self-indulgence, late nights on Red Bull, under-exercising or obsessive exercising, we need to ask ourselves if we are serving God with our bodies. We need to care for them properly: with sleep, exercise, sensible meals and balanced diets.

But what about how we look – grooming and style and fashion? Peter and Paul both have words to say about them too.

### Nurturing outward modesty and inner beauty

Peter, writing to wives of unbelieving husbands, says:

> Your beauty should not come from outward adornment, such as braided hair and the wearing of gold jewellery and fine clothes. Instead, it should be that of your inner self, the unfading beauty of a gentle and quiet spirit, which is of great worth in God's sight. For this is the way the holy women of the past who put their hope in God used to make themselves beautiful.
>
> (1 Peter 3:3–5 NIV)

Does that mean literally no gold jewellery? No hair braiding? The former warden of Tyndale House, a biblical research library in Cambridge, told me that he once read these descriptions to a classical scholar. He asked, 'What does that mean to you?' She said at once, 'He's telling them not to dress like upper-class prostitutes.'[15] Other scholars think he's critiquing extravagant clothes and over-elaborate hairstyles. It could well be a bit of both – drawing attention to oneself; ostentation; perhaps in order to seduce, to look sexy.

> I also want women to dress *modestly*, with decency and propriety, not with braided hair or gold or pearls or expensive clothes, but with good deeds.
>
> (1 Timothy 2:9–10 NIV, emphasis mine)

It doesn't mean dressing frumpily, but it does mean watching out that you don't reveal too much flesh. It doesn't mean dressing untidily, but it does mean you won't make fashion your idol. It doesn't mean we can't buy nice clothes, but it does mean that we aren't extravagant or ostentatious with them.

Later in 1 Timothy, Paul reminds us that God richly provides us with everything for our enjoyment. That surely applies to clothes and hairstyles. They are a way of expressing personality and enjoying God's good gifts. It is surely right for us to express our personality through well-chosen clothes and hairstyles. We are free not to conform to stereotypes; God loves variety.

But there is more. Both Paul and Peter say that the priority is caring for the inner life and making that beautiful and expressing it in good works. Peter observes something intriguing. He says *that* was how Sarah, Rebecca and Rachel made themselves beautiful. The Old Testament calls them beautiful. But this was their secret: nurturing inner beauty which showed in outward love.

As we gaze at Jesus, we will be transformed. As we nurture our inner life by fixing our lives on Jesus, as we look outward to others, seeing how we can love them and serve them with good deeds, we will be transformed.

> Sometimes the key to finding freedom from our struggles with the beauty culture is in discovering that we've been paying way too much attention to ourselves and not enough attention to loving others.[16]

Louisa May Alcott said, 'Love is a great beautifier.'[17] Interestingly, she is best known as the author of *Little Women*, and was someone with huge insight into women's hearts. I think she is completely right and that is why so many older Christian's faces are so profoundly beautiful. I look at my older church members as they leave at the end of our service each Sunday morning and I see great beauty in their faces. They have received a great deal of love and given a great deal of love – and it shows. As one leader puts it, 'Grace can make what nature has given us even more beautiful.'[18]

## Being careful what we see

We need to watch what we watch and filter what we see. Images affect us. In a survey, 70% of women felt depressed, guilty and shameful after looking at a fashion magazine for only three minutes. If you're among them – you don't have to look at that stuff!

Men are also affected by images. Research indicates that men shown pictures of *Playboy* models later describe themselves as less in love with their wives than men shown other images. There are many reasons why viewing pornography is harmful. It rots your soul. It enslaves you. It degrades your inner sexuality.[19] It distorts your view of women. And it affects in a truly harmful and dysfunctional way your relationship with your future girlfriend and wife. It's not just porn, but also films and magazines which include idealized and airbrushed images of people. Seeing them has an effect. We can't avoid them completely, but we can try – and we can be aware of the effect they have. We need to look at others differently.

## Olivia's story

Michelle Graham tells the story of her friend Olivia. Olivia struggled to love her body most of her life. She felt huge pressure to look good in front of her colleagues. One weekend she was away on a work conference. Her alarm clock didn't go off. She lost thirty minutes of primping time.

As she looked at her reflection in the mirror, she blurted out to God, 'Why do I have to care so much about what they think of me?'

She was surprised by the response she sensed from the Lord: 'You don't.'

'What do you mean, I don't?' she snapped.

What she felt God saying was this: 'It really is your choice. You can choose whose opinion matters to you. Today, choose mine. I love you. And I think you're exquisite.'

Olivia began to realize that it was sin to value others' opinion of her over God's. It was sin to reject the body God had graciously made for her. It was sin to crave the praise of other people. And she had a choice in the matter.[20]

So do we.

### God is merciful

Paul makes his appeal for us to please God with our bodies 'by the mercies of God'. Isn't that wonderful? We insult God by making our hair an idol, by caring more about grooming than praying in the morning. We rebel against him by idolizing our bodies. We end up in the misery of sin. And he says, 'Come back to me.'

He is so merciful. We aren't. We are perfectionist and unmerciful. We refuse to accept ourselves.

He says, 'I accept you. In Christ. He has paid for all your sin. He is the perfection you lack. And he is yours. You are in him.'

He is so much more merciful to you than you are to yourself. You say, 'I hate my body.'

He says, 'I don't. I love it.'

He is so merciful and he loves being pleased. You say, 'My body's not good enough.'

He replies: 'Says who? Looks fine to me. I made it. I like it that way. Now stop worrying so much about it! You'll never please me if you're so obsessed with how you look. Look at my Son instead. Think of others instead. In view of my kindness to you, offer me your body as a living sacrifice, holy and pleasing to me.'

## For discussion or personal reflection
Read Romans 12:1–2.

1. Have you ever seen that these verses apply to personal appearance and body image?
2. How would you apply them to the way you feel about your own body and appearance?
3. How are you tempted to make an idol of your appearance? Why?
4. What are the implications for your self-image of Jesus 'being nothing special to look at'?
5. What can you do practically in terms of how you look at others or what pictures you look at? Why is this important?

The way the word 'idol' is used most often in everyday, non-religious settings today is for people. Almost always it is a description of someone famous: a Premier League football player, a pop singer, a film star. TV chiefs called their talent show *Pop Idol* in an attempt to cash in on this usage. For once copying us, rather than the other way round, the Americans produced *American Idol*.

## Robbie, Jade, Paris and Diana

At its most crass, this tendency to look up to celebrities saw footballer player Robbie Fowler given the nickname 'God' by the crowd at Anfield, Liverpool's ground. Sometimes the idols are people who through odd circumstances become famous for, er, being famous – like Jade Goody or Paris Hilton. Sometimes there is a Princess Diana figure who is thrust into the limelight reluctantly, but learns to manipulate it to become the defining celebrity idol of modern times. Apparently some people still worship her as the reincarnation of the goddess Diana or a messianic figure who will return one day.[1]

## Why 'people idols'?

In a moment I want to think about the way we idolize people we actually know. But first, it's worth considering what is happening in the modern cult (another religious word) of celebrity.[2] The whole thing is, of course, a media creation with three interested parties: the media (largely red-top newspapers and glossy magazines), who sell lots of copies; the celebrities themselves, who may simply enjoy the public exposure or may profit from it too; and the idolizers, like you and me.

I hadn't been to a rock concert since I was a teenager. On an impulse I got tickets to see Bruce Springsteen. It was an extraordinary experience. To be honest, the sound wasn't great: it was the first concert in Arsenal football club's new Emirates stadium and the sound mix could have been better. But there was a rare and powerful sense of being part of something different. 'The Boss' played the crowd, projecting a sense of personal warmth that felt entirely genuine and creating a wonderful sense of community. I found it easy to see why people followed him around, comparing notes on the internet and paying vast amounts of money in pursuit of this elusive something. I also saw that it was a pathway to 'idolatry'.

Why do we idolize these people? They are our representatives, giving us a sense of ourselves as we might be. We identify ourselves with them, enjoying the sense of being part of something big, glamorous, successful and stylish. Our own identities are fragile: we project onto our idol what we think would give us stability and happiness.

Joan's life was a bit dull: a job as an office assistant which she had mastered and was bored by; a husband pre-occupied with snooker; kids who never worked at school and looked as though they'd never work after it. Her looks had been OK when she was eighteen, but she'd rather let herself go after her pregnancies had left her with a tummy like a big marshmallow. The highlight of her week was buying *Hello* magazine: she loved to see Victoria Beckham or Kelly Brook out in the latest fashions, and she liked catching up with all the gossip too – who had dumped whom, who had been caught with whom . . . for a few minutes she forgot herself in the glamour of others.

### Football and violence

Football in particular draws out of men a level of commitment and emotion that often amazes the women in their lives. We see the high level of devotion in the successes, failures and most of all perceived injustices on the pitch. It is so high because the idol becomes the figurehead of a whole sense of belonging and identity, the representative of a community. When there is a threat, deep-seated, primal defence mechanisms kick in:

> There is no reason for surprise that the ecstasies of a crowd of sporting fans are so often violent. The self-esteem of any social body has a demon inhabiting it, which may always break out when there are no structures of responsibility.[3]

### Christians and celebrity idols

Christians need to be on their guard against this cult of celebrity because they are not immune from any form of idolatry. What are we reading? Why? What is happening to us as we follow the chaotic antics of a Britney Spears? What does our level of interest show us about ourselves? Poring over the scandalous or trivial details of celebrities we are never likely to meet – is that really a morally neutral behaviour?

We also need to watch for our own version of celebrity idols in the church. Churches are remarkably vulnerable to personality cults. Instant access to sermons on line (not generally a bad thing, I hasten to add) has fed this.[4] Strong natural leaders with good speaking skills and something edgy or controversial to say are idolized and put in the place of Christ. We assume that if Dr X has pronounced on something, then that is right; or we feel that if only Pastor Y is speaking at our mission or conference, then everything will go well.

### Don't put the vicar on a pedestal!

People also idolize their own leaders. In a profound analysis, Simon Walker suggests that congregations tend to relate unhelpfully to leaders through a process called 'idealization'. It is more commonly called 'hero worship'. We cope with our own sense of inadequacy by burying it and looking for someone else 'through whom to live a surrogate life'. We choose someone who can be strong in the areas where we are weak. We may be failing to pray, but if they are praying, somehow all is well. Our witness may be virtually non-existent, but if she can share stories of evangelistic encounters, that somehow compensates for it. 'And so we idealize ordinary people who have taken up the burden of leadership and turn them into the ideal heroes we need them to be.' We seek the wholeness we lack not in Christ, but in our vicar.

### A dodgy deal

What does that do to the poor man or woman? Our leaders very often sense the adulation and try to meet the standards we have set for them. They, of course, are far from perfect, but they have to hide their imperfections on the 'back stage' of their life, showing only the strengths and successes their people need to see. It creates a dysfunctional deal 'in which both parties meet their needs through the other'.[5]

Think about your church leaders for a moment. What are your expectations of them? Have you idealized them in an attempt to compensate for your own shortcomings? Are you prepared to let them be real people, or must they exist in your mind as spiritual superstars?

Geoff was bowled over by the church he was taken to by the second-year students from his hall. It made his family's parish church at home seem rather quaint. Great music, big crowds, and what a preacher: so cool, so witty, so contemporary with his spiked hair and Converse boots! Geoff's own attempts to pray seemed so feeble, but he felt better when the leader described his long conversations with God.

### Repenting of our Christian idols

Think about your attitude to well-known Christian speakers and even personalities. Does listening to so many of their talks or reading their books have any downsides? Are you making adverse comparisons with the sermons you hear in the flesh each week? Does the preacher on the TV seem to have better illustrations, funnier jokes, more moving stories and a better way of explaining the passage than the flesh-and-blood preacher who stands at the front week in, week out? Do you plan your attendance at Christian conferences and events largely on the basis of whether the speaker is well known and successful?

## Relational idols

We began this book with my account of how I had allowed my girlfriend (as she then was) to eclipse Jesus in my heart. As I have read, preached and talked with people over the years about relationships, I have become sure that my experience is not an isolated one, but a very typical pattern of idolatrous behaviour.

### Robbie's search

Robbie Williams has a song called 'A Love Supreme', borrowing the title of a jazz piece by John Coltrane. In it he sings of people searching for a relationship but unable to find one, among other reasons, either because they have become over-weight and baggy-eyed, or because the best-looking men 'are all gay'. He describes the search through place after place for a 'love supreme', the need to avoid love songs which whisper that love will stop the pain and kill the fear. He concludes that everyone 'lives for love'.

### Amazing idolatry

This is the road to idolatry, a road along which many have travelled further than Robbie Williams.[6] Take John Newton, for instance. Yes, *the* John Newton, the ex-slave-trader who got converted, became a vicar, wrote 'Amazing Grace', and helped (eventually) in the anti-slave-trade campaign of 1787–1807 led by William Wilberforce. In one of his letters, Newton writes about his marriage and confesses a danger of which everyone seeking or in a relationship needs to be aware:

> I am now far advanced in the twenty-fifth year of marriage;
> and I set out blindfold and was so far infatuated by an idolatrous
> passion, that for a while I looked no higher for happiness than
> to a worm like myself [that is – to his wife!].[7]

It sounds remarkably like something Robbie Williams could have written, though more precisely analysed. Newton looked for happiness only in his wife. He calls her a 'worm' not to be rude (after all, he says he is a worm too): his point is that she is not God, but he is investing all his hopes in her.

## Not a very good Lord of Lords

The same pattern could be seen in Michelle Graham's relationship:

> I looked to [my husband] to make me feel loved, to keep me from loneliness, to make me happy when I wasn't, to give me wise advice, to help me grow spiritually . . . the list went on. And while those things are often benefits of a healthy relationship, God did not put him in my life to fulfil my needs, otherwise I wouldn't need God anymore. I also found that my husband didn't make a very good Lord of Lords.
>
> At first I got frustrated with him. He wasn't meeting my needs. He wasn't fulfilling his husbandly duties. Then God reminded me that my expectations for him were unfair. Of course he couldn't do for me what only God could do. I needed to let go of desire to be fulfilled by my husband and replace it with desire for God.[8]

## The idol pattern

Notice the pattern: high expectations followed by disappointment and frustration. It is played out again and again in relationships, because we project onto our girlfriend or husband hopes that only God can meet. We make of that person an idol; and he or she inevitably disappoints us.

Sometimes the other person collaborates with the idolatry by trying to meet those expectations. He or she inevitably fails and then has that to deal with too. Sometimes the other person refuses and backs off, leaving the relationship in a fragile state. Either way, the idolatry is destructive.

### Making him or her God

At root, relational idolatry is based on expecting a person to take the place of God. It is unfair, idolatrous and downright daft. No-one can do that. No-one needs to! God is there, wanting to be God to us. Why impose that impossible burden on an ordinary fallen human being like your wife or husband?

### Recovery

Psychologist Herman Hendrix has spent a lifetime observing and trying to help troubled marriages. He observes:

> Many people come to the sobering conclusion that what they want most from their partners is what their partners are least able to give.[9]

He doesn't use the language of idolatry, but what he sees is surely representative of it. Hendrix responded to the problem by developing a kind of marriage therapy called 'Imago Therapy', which apparently many couples have found helpful.

But Hendrix never really answers the question underlying the troubled relationship and its problems: 'Who will make me whole? Who can heal me?' It is one thing to recognize that my wife can't be my messiah, but that still leaves me messiah-less! The best marriage therapy in the world isn't going to make my wife able to satisfy all my needs. And if I don't put all my hopes in her, where will they go? The only answer can be God. It is as we put God in his right place that our relationships can grow in healthy ways.

### How God rescued Newton from wife worship

This is what seems to have happened to John Newton over time as God led him along some hard paths:

The Lord . . . did not deal with me as I deserved. He sent, indeed, again and again, a worm to the root of my gourd, and many an anxious trembling hour have I suffered; but he pitied my weakness, gradually opened my eyes and while he in some measure weakened and mortified [i.e. put to death] the idolatrous part of affection, he smiles upon that part of it which was lawful, and caused it to flourish and strengthen from year to year.[10]

Notice how he traces God's hand in his life. First, God is gracious: 'he did not deal with me as I deserved'. God does not give us our just deserts, even for our idolatry. What a relief! Next, God sends him suffering. Yes, that is what Newton sees as God's response to his idolatry: hard times.

### Mrs Newton is indisposed

He uses a rather quaint picture for his suffering: 'he sent a worm to the root of my gourd'. This comes from Jonah 4, where the prophet is sheltering from the sun under the leaves of a vine (or gourd) and the vine withers. Jonah gets very hot and feels lousy. Newton gives no details, but having read through his letters, I have a hunch that he is referring to his wife's poor health, which he often writes about. I suspect that God used her frequent illnesses to wean Newton away from his 'idolatrous passion' (this may well mean making sex within marriage an idol) for his wife and to help him learn to look to God to be his happiness.

He wrote to one friend at a time when his wife was ill:

As he is tender, he is wise also: he loves us, but especially with regard to our best interests. If there were not something in our hearts and our situation that required discipline and medicine, he so delights in our prosperity, that we should never be in heaviness. The innumerable comforts and mercies with which he enriches

even those we call darker days, are sufficient proofs that he
does not willingly grieve us; but when he sees a need-be for
chastisement, he will not withhold it because he loves us; on
the contrary, that is the very reason why he afflicts. He will put
his silver into the fire to purify it; but he sits by the furnace as a
refiner, to direct the process, and to secure the end he has in view,
that we may neither suffer too much nor suffer in vain.[11]

### Testing for idols

Back to the present! If you are married or in a relationship,
what expectations do you have of your 'other half'? Are they
in any way idolatrous?

If you want a test, then look for excessive reactions when
the other person lets you down or disappoints you in some
way: they are late; they embarrass you in public; they don't
want to have sex; they aren't much interested in your day or
even your problems; they don't want to go out; they are ill
and can't give you their normal level of attention, support or
practical help. It's natural to be a bit disappointed with any of
these, but idolatry produces an excessive emotional reaction.
We may show it or keep it to ourselves. But that is the test.

Gillian's mother had died when she was six. It left her
lonely and insecure. Throughout sixth form she only felt
happy when there was a man on her arm. At the end of
her first term at university, Andrew asked her out. She
was delighted. But when he forgot he was taking her to
the cinema and went out with his mates to watch football
in the pub, she exploded and then collapsed in tears.
Afterwards she wondered why she'd reacted like that. It
wasn't even as though he was that great a catch anyway,
as her friend pointed out!

# Family idols

I have concentrated on romantic relationships and marriage here. However, people don't impose messiah-like expectations only on girlfriends. We can see our parents that way. Or our children or grandchildren. Or our family as a whole: the dream of the perfect family, like a mixture of *The Waltons* and *Little House on the Prairie*.[12] Excessive and inappropriate hopes that they must meet our needs for practical help, companionship or meaning distort many of these close relationships.

## *Parents idolizing children*

Parents need to be alert from the earliest days of parenthood in case they may idolize their children. This doesn't necessarily mean being too lax and indulgent, though very often it does. It can be seen in excessively harsh and restrictive parenting. Behind it lies a need for control; a desire to live my life through my children; a hope that I can compensate for my failures by making them perfect. In an odd way, I am simultaneously putting myself in the place of God *and* making them into little idols to meet my needs!

> Nigel and Louise had been married for two years and already Nigel's mother was clucking. Every time they visited, the conversation eventually got round to babies. After a while Louise found it so oppressive that she let Nigel go on his own. Nigel's mother wondered why the daughter-in-law she adored was avoiding her.

## *Idols and family break-up*

Parents may hope their children *won't* marry because they don't want to lose them. Or they may make it all too plain that they *must* get married and produce grandchildren: thus fulfilling their need for status, approval or companionship. Commentators often lament the breakdown of the extended family in contemporary Britain, for example. I wonder how much it is due to idolatrous expectations that drive families apart. Even where the results are not catastrophic, they can be claustrophobic and uncomfortable – the duty trip to Granny who demands it in the most unreasonable circumstances.

## Idols in friendships

Friendships can also become idolatrous. Often there is a buried, or not so buried, romantic or sexual attraction present, but not always. Sometimes there is simply a very high degree of dependency which is far in excess of the other person's ability to deliver. Expectations rocket sky high; they are inevitably disappointed; tension and difficulties result. Psychologists have their own language and explanations for this, but the Bible would see a pattern of idolatry. The answer is repentance, forgiveness and learning to put God where he should be.

## For discussion or personal reflection

1.  Are you excessively interested in tabloid celebrities? Or over-committed to a sports team? Where does that come from? Is it honouring to God?
2.  Think about your attitude to your local church leader. Do you idealize that person? Is that good for either side?
3.  What about your use of internet sermons or Christian conferences: does it affect your attitude to your pastor's preaching in an unhelpful way?
4.  Consider a key relationship in your life. It may be with your boy- or girlfriend, husband or wife, or with another family member or friend. What are your expectations for comfort, support, companionship and

identity? Have you put that person onto God's throne? How does it show?

5. Think of the relationships you dream of – a wife or child or friend, perhaps. What are your hopes? Are you idolizing what you are longing for?

6. Now read Ephesians 1:3–14. What has God given you in Christ that you are looking for in people?

## 7. RELIGIOUS AND CHURCH IDOLS

Idolatry in the Bible was first and foremost about wrong *images* of God. We must not lose sight of this primary focus, even though it is right to see all sorts of non-religious items as potential idols.[1] So many of the early Christians had been idol worshippers, bowing down to actual statues in temples. Paul reminded his Thessalonian friends how they 'turned . . . from idols to serve the living and true God' (1 Thessalonians 1:9). He had to work through with the believers in Corinth whether they could keep going to idol temples and even eat meat that had been offered there.

### Idol statues today

For some readers, this will be an issue with which you can identify very closely. An old Christian friend of mine, and a fellow minister, obtained a PhD from the University of Aberdeen for a thesis about the powers of evil and idols in 1 Corinthians. In his acknowledgments he wrote:

> The origins of the topic of this thesis, the relationship between evil powers and idols, go back to my Zoroastrian background. The issue is not merely an academic one, but a profoundly existential one for me and for millions of Christians round the world, who ponder the problems of food offered to idols on a regular basis. I have wrestled in thought, prayer, and practice with the problem of food offered to idols.[2]

In our congregation in central Cambridge there are often young Asian students who have to wrestle with the issue of reverence for ancestors in the context of Asian religions. Should they join their parents in offering gifts and prayers?

Paul's guidance on this issue is spelt out in 1 Corinthians 8 and 10. Essentially, what he says seems to rule out attendance at pagan worship occasions where there is idol worship. Though idols may be empty and dumb, evil spiritual forces use them to get a hold on people, so going to their temple to join in with a time of worship is dangerous. I cannot claim any first-hand experience of these kinds of issues, though members of my congregation have such. What I would advise is to handle such situations with great humility and courtesy, because the effect of non-involvement is likely to be offensive or incomprehensible.[3] But we have to remain true to Christ.

Sanjay's family had moved from India to Walsall in the 1950s. They were Hindus – well, at least in theory, though his mother was pretty devout. In his second year at university he started going to a small group run by some Christians. Over time he found himself drawn to Jesus almost as if by a magnetic force. When he went home for the holidays his mother took no notice of his new faith . . . until it came to the next family wedding.

## Idol thoughts of God

In our age, how we feel so often determines what we are willing to believe. It is so common to hear people say, 'I could never believe in a God who . . . ' At that point we are committing idolatry. We are making a god: we are not receiving the revelation of the one true God and believing it.

It is possible to commit idolatry by the way we think about God – making him into something different from what he is and worshipping that. Such man-made gods are idols of the mind. Listen to these words from A. W. Tozer:

> Let us beware lest we in our pride accept the erroneous notion that idolatry consists only in kneeling down before visible objects of adoration, and that civilized peoples are therefore free from it. The essence of idolatry is the entertainment of thoughts about God that are unworthy of him.[4]

## Is ignorance idolatry?

Any thought about God that is inaccurate or unworthy is an act of idolatry. It is a false God, not the true one. We immediately meet some difficulties: none of us has a perfect understanding of the Bible, and what we know of God can modify over time as more light breaks forth from his word. We may begin the Christian life with very little understanding of his eternal purposes, for example. Over time we see it more clearly. That is not a movement from idolatry – it is just normal Christian growth.

## Man-made God

What we mean by this mind of idolatry is someone wilfully rejecting the Bible's view of God, either on one specific area or as a whole, preferring to devise his or her own God to worship.

Here are some possibilities. We may refuse to believe in a God who judges people for their sin. We may say we cannot accept the Bible's teaching about a God who punishes sin. We may object violently to the idea that God chooses some people for salvation and not others. It is interesting to look at this last one, because Paul gives us his reaction to that objection.

What then shall we say? Is God unjust? Not at all! For he says to
Moses,

'I will have mercy on whom I have mercy,

and I will have compassion on whom I have compassion.'
It does not, therefore, depend on human desire or effort, but on
God's mercy. For Scripture says to Pharaoh: 'I raised you up for
this very purpose, that I might display my power in you and that
my name might be proclaimed in all the earth.' Therefore God
has mercy on whom he wants to have mercy, and he hardens
whom he wants to harden.
(Romans 9:14–18)

Now that sounds pretty hard, doesn't it? We read that at our
family prayer time and eyebrows were raised round the table.
Inevitably someone asked how it could be fair. I had to say
that all I could do was to read on:

One of you will say to me: 'Then why does God still blame
us? For who is able to resist his will?' But who are you, a mere
human being, to talk back to God? 'Shall what is formed say
to the one who formed it, "Why did you make me like this?"'
Does not the potter have the right to make out of the same lump
of clay some pottery for noble purposes and some for disposal of
refuse?

What if God, although choosing to show his wrath and make
his power known, bore with great patience the objects of his
wrath – prepared for destruction?
(Romans 9:19–22)

With hard doctrines, we have a choice. We can believe them,
or we can adjust them. If we believe them, we give God
glory and treat him as God. If we adjust them, we commit
idolatry.

## Jesus is OK for you, but . . .

One particularly current issue is religious pluralism. To say that one religion is better than another has become almost a criminal offence in the UK. Not quite. But almost. It is definitely right at the top of the possible political correctness crimes. I am not for a moment trying to claim the right to insult other religions gratuitously. That would not be very Christian. I do want them to be able to try to explain their distinctive teachings in a clear and persuasive way. And I want the same right for myself – because the Bible itself is so clear about the uniqueness of Jesus Christ. *Jesus* is clear about it, for goodness' sake, saying, 'I am the way and the truth and the life. No-one comes to the Father except through me' (John 14:6).

> The college chaplain did his best to involve every possible kind of Christian in chapel activities. He stressed the inclusiveness of the gospel. During Women's Awareness Week, he invited members of the Women's Group Spirituality Caucus to lead the evening Compline service. Jane went along a little nervously. The service began with an invocation: 'Mother God – we acknowledge you as the World Spirit, present in all religions, slave of none.' Jane felt even more nervous and looked at the chaplain.

## That's just how it is for me

At a mission to Oxford University in 1984, the then Archbishop of Canterbury quoted the first half of that verse from John 14:6, stopping at 'the life'. He then added, 'At least, that is how it is for me.' A local minister said afterwards that he could barely restrain himself from shouting out, 'Complete the quotation!' To say that Jesus is not 'the only name under heaven by which we must be saved' (see Acts 4:12) is to create an idol.

We must beware, though, of sitting in judgment on others whose deviation from sound doctrine is more obvious. We can make our own versions of God by emphasizing, say, his love so that his judgment never gets mentioned, or his holiness so that grace recedes out of sight. We too can make the God we want by picking and choosing what we like in the Bible – and end up with an idol.

## The idol of religious performance

If there is anything more dangerous than irreligion, it is probably religion! Many respectable people who believe in God believe just as strongly that their own prayers and religious observance will get them to heaven. Their own religious performance becomes their idol.

Is that you? What are you trusting to save you – your church attendance or Christ's death, your charitable giving or the grace of God? As a teenager it took me eighteen months to realize that the religion of personal effort I had developed for myself was not working and, actually, it didn't have to – just believing in Jesus would get me to heaven!

Esther's home wasn't Christian, but it was moral and God-fearing. In her first job she went through a hard time and started praying again. She gave more money to charity and tried to be kind to those around her. Somehow it didn't seem to bring her very close to God – or to change her very much on the inside. She found herself looking rather wistfully at her younger sister, who 'found Jesus' at university and seemed much more relaxed about life.

## Idolatry in service

Even for those who believe in salvation by grace, Christian service can become an idol. There is a real danger in the ways we serve God in church, in prayer, Bible study, leadership, evangelism and other church or 'Christian' activities.[5] This is particularly true of pastors, vicars and others paid to work for churches and Christian organizations. We address these 'full-time' ministry idols below, but I would invite you to read the section even if you are not in that line of work yourself. There are three reasons. First, it will help you understand and help your own church leaders. Second, it may well remind you of your own drives to overwork in your own personal calling. Finally, much of it may well apply to your own unpaid 'Christian service' in church or other Christian groups.

The idol of high performance is too often on the window sill in front of a *pastor's* desk. Many Tuesday mornings, as I start a new week,[6] I present last Sunday's sermon hoping that I have pleased my idol with what I have achieved. If the sermon felt a bit substandard – solidly biblical, perhaps, but lacking in bite or interest – then the idol stares at me sadly and I feel a failure.

The pain is the result of idolatry on my part. It is as if I have dragged a stone statue into the centre of the temple and bowed down to it. At the heart of my life's work, I have let myself become enslaved in the service of an idol or two. The idols of my own performance and reputation have taken centre stage.

Ministry idols show themselves in other ways. One is overwork. Ministry idols are harder taskmasters than Christ. Ministry idols want our exclusive attention. Ministry idols are intensely jealous. Ministry idols don't let us take rest days. Ministry idols weave their own patterns of magic, their own enticing delusional fields. They make eighty-hour weeks for pastors with young children seem so natural and right. Ministry idols persuade us that as council members or Sunday school teachers we are completely indispensable. 'You are the best,' they whisper flatteringly. 'Don't delegate the children's talk to anyone else – it won't be nearly as good as if you do it.'

Ministry idols are particularly unhappy about your devotion to your church being shared with your family. 'Family?' they murmur to you. 'Don't let them be a distraction.' If you baulk at that, then ministry idols have proof-texts up their sleeves, which they produce like a poker player with a winning ace. 'Come on,' they whisper, 'remember what Jesus said. You have to hate your wife and children if you are going to follow him.'

In her marvellous history of Christian mission, *From Jerusalem to Irian Jaya*, Ruth Tucker tells the story of Bob Pierce. He was a youth evangelist. After visiting a missionary orphanage in China in 1947, he felt God's call to help the poor: 'From that point on his energy was devoted to Christian humanitarianism.'[7] He became a 'saintly legend throughout the Far East'. He travelled round the USA raising vast sums for new hospitals, orphanages and other ministries. But he neglected his family.

> It was during this rapid time of growth for World Vision that Lorraine [his wife] and the girls seemed to be pushed further and further away from the top of Bob's priority list. When he did return to his family from his average of ten months of travel a year, it was almost as though he was a visitor in his own home, and conflict inevitably ensued. Though he could sympathetically relate to the world, his own family living under his own roof seemed so far away.[8]

Later one of his daughters committed suicide and Bob had a breakdown. Tucker concludes: 'He had become further alienated from his family, and never again would they enjoy a sustained happy relationship.'[9]

How can this possibly happen? A dangerous but highly plausible line for us to take goes like this. I tell myself that my wife is there to make my ministry happen. 'That's *her* ministry – supporting you,' coos the idol, sounding ever so spiritual. 'Take charge, man. You wouldn't want her to sin by deflecting you from your important ministry, would you?' Ministry idols are quite happy to enlist new worshippers, so they are keen to recruit your spouse and children into the cult of ministry.

Even more subtly, ministry idols may manage to fool you that your relationship with your children is about making them into ministers too. In her novel *Oranges Are Not the Only Fruit*, Jeannette Winterson portrays a young girl adopted by Christian parents in the north of England. From an early age they told her that her life was to be spent as a missionary in China. Winterson has admitted that the novel was closely autobiographical. Unsurprisingly, she rebelled against the Christian faith.

Ministry idols also affect your leadership style. Because your church plant is so important, it is obvious to the ministry idol that everyone must work as hard as you, or feel inferior and be made to feel inferior. Ministry idols love to have ministers who lead their whole church in worship – of the idol, of course. So homes where one or other parent is out at church activities five nights a week are spiritual homes.

Dora grew up in a Christian home. There was a lot of love and they went to a good church where she was taught the Bible faithfully every week. She loved her mum and dad. Her dad was a deacon in the church. Most nights her dad got the train home from Birmingham, flew through the door, ate dinner and then rushed out for a meeting. She sometimes wished he could spend a bit of time playing with her or helping with her homework.

## Not just the pastor

I would not want to give the impression that it is only paid Christian leaders who worship ministry idols. Let me give an example. You may be one of the pillars of the church – your speciality, perhaps, is catering. The vicar said last September that harvest suppers would not be harvest suppers without your quiches. This year, however, your mother had a fall. She needs a lot more of your time. Time for quiche-making is as rare as rain in the Sahara. You have to hand control of the catering team over to your deputy.

In that moment, you are embarrassed at how angry you feel with your mother for falling over and depriving you of your fun. For a moment you wish she had died instead. Then you check yourself and wonder what is going on. Seize that moment. That is a crucial moment. A moment of insight and illumination. A moment when the curtains are parted and your heart is more visible to you than it usually is. Grab hold of those feelings and ask God to help you understand how much they are based on ministry idols that have been denied their usual worship and are wreaking their revenge on your emotions.

I feel particularly humbled in writing this section because I have lived so much of it. The breakdown I had in 2006, which meant five months off work, was partly caused by overwork and anxiety about ministry. Underlying the overwork and the anxiety were a shelf of ministry idols that needed exposing through skilled help. I am still working on busting them, though!

## Idols in church life

Here are some more ways in which local church life can be affected – or perhaps the word should be 'infected' – with idolatry.

### The omnicompetent pastor

Sometimes pastors try to do everything. It is tempting for them to try to be omnicompetent – able to preach, lead services, see people pastorally, chair meetings, lead the outreach groups, be hands on with the youth work, produce the bulletins. I knew one country vicar who resigned because he even had to mow the graveyard! It may also be very tempting for the congregation, who feel that they are getting their money's worth – and don't have to miss an episode of *Coronation Street* or a Champion's League match. But it simply isn't biblical (see Romans 12:3–8; 1 Corinthians 12:4–31).

### Idols of tradition

Long-standing ways of doing things become entrenched. To change them seems risky: we trust our traditions – but we need to ask whether our devotion to our precious way of doing things is really biblical. Jesus had to rebuke people like this. 'You have a fine way of setting aside the commands of God in order to keep your own traditions,' he said to the Pharisees (see Matthew 15:6). The way to detect an idol of tradition is when people say, 'But we've always done it this way', as if that settled things. Tradition has its uses, but it can also be an idol.

### Novelty idols

The opposite to traditionalism is the idol of novelty. Our cultural moment prizes novelty: there is a strong tendency to think that new ideas or methods will improve things. We do need to respond to changes in society and ensure we are as culturally relevant as we can be, but often this goes too far and churches are led by faddishness. I see new fads (usually but not always from California!) crashing over British church life in great waves on a depressingly regular basis. We are made to feel that if we aren't surfing each new wave we are finished. Actually, we are being invited to worship at the altar of novelty. One church leader had a phrase he used constantly: 'moving on'. In the end some of his church began to ask what it was they were moving on to. It didn't seem to matter terribly. What counted was 'moving on'.

### Technique and technology idols

Ours is a technocratic age, offering astonishing technical advances and a devotion to fine-tuning techniques. Electronic screens, live internet streaming of sermons, PowerPoint presentations – they are all great servants, but dangerous masters. When churches trust the technology or the technique rather than the Lord, these things become idols.

### The idol of success

Sometimes people ask me how many people come to my church. I am ashamed to say I have developed 'Minister Maths'. You see, preachers have their own funny way of counting. It goes like this. Think of the number of people in your congregation and add 25%. Then add another 10–15 people just to be sure. Why? Because we serve an idol called success. We have to have good numbers and we must be growing. Even more important is that we must be seen to be growing. We have fallen victim to the Success Syndrome. One leader of an innovative small church which has seen many people converted from difficult backgrounds was told he wouldn't be asked to speak at a Christian conference because his church didn't have several hundred people in it. That made me sad, because I know that many apparently successful churches may actually have relatively few converts among their new members.

### Emotion

That may sound like an odd idol, but it is a very real one in our day in many churches. It is closely linked to music – and to speaking as well. The aim of the service or the celebration is to produce an emotional high. The sermon's goal is to get people laughing or crying. There is a very real need for emotional engagement with God, but it is always feeling based on truth, driven by the great facts of sin and the message of salvation.[10] To try to whip up feeling through music or preaching is manipulative – and almost always a result of an idolization of feeling.

### Conclusion

Beware religious idols! We can forsake 'worldly' idols, but become ensnared and spiritually lost in 'spiritual' ones instead.

## For discussion or personal reflection

Read Ephesians 1:3–8.

1. What is hard to accept in this passage? In which ways do you see people, including yourself, tempted to alter the biblical doctrine of God? Why is this such a serious thing?

2. What do these verses have to say to our feeling that we have to earn God's favour? How does that affect us when we are asked to take on an additional responsibility in church or Christian Union for which we don't really have time?

3. If Ephesians is about identity, where does Paul see our identity coming from in these verses? How does this impinge on your service in church or Christian organizations?

4. Take some time to meditate on your motives for service and your secret hopes and fears about being asked to be in a particular ministry. Why do you 'need' to do it or be asked to do it?

## 8. POLITICAL, INTELLECTUAL AND CULTURAL IDOLS

Almost anything can be an idol – not simply cars, jobs and relationships. Idolatry pervades every part of human living. In this chapter we look at some idols in the arenas of politics, ideas and culture. It may not seem like your kind of thing and if you find it hard going, I'd encourage you to skip it for now.

### Political idols

It would be easy to start with misplaced passion: being over-committed to political goals or leaders or parties. But I want to begin in a different place: with political indifference and disengagement. One of the worrying features of our times is the way that our politics (I am speaking about the UK here) has turned people off. Single-issue concerns like global warming or economic fairness get our juices flowing. Politics as such leaves us reaching for the remote. Recent scandals in the UK have further deepened our collective cynicism.

It may seem odd, but there is another kind of idol being worshipped here. When you look at the crying needs of so many poor and underprivileged people in our world, you have to wonder if one of the greatest sins being committed is worship of the idol of cynicism – a refusal to engage with a faulty political process to make the best of it that we can.

### Other potential idols

Perhaps the two great causes of our time are international development and global warming. Both are driven by powerful moral imperatives and real issues. The underlying values – concern for the poor and the environment – are deeply biblical ones. Three visits to Sierra Leone have involved me in meeting some of the very poorest people in the world. Statistically their prospects are grim. Who cannot be concerned for their welfare?

Understanding the effects of human greenhouse gas emissions raises huge fears for the poor (for they are the ones most at risk from global warming) as well as for the rest of us – and for the natural world. But without in any way downplaying the urgency of both issues, we need to be aware that both will inevitably generate idolatrous attitudes and behaviours.

A commitment to contain global warming may become all-obsessive, particularly in relation to other human needs. The earth can become god-like, rather than simply a part of the created universe.

For some churches, social action virtually displaces the Christ-given mission to explain the gospel to non-Christians. We may be drawn into operating with the liberal humanist assumption that there is nothing much wrong with our hearts, and that through good will, education, organization and technology we can fix things. This ignores the realities of the selfishness of the human heart.[1] When I have asked Africans about the biggest need their countries have if they are to grow out of poverty, they have all said immediately, 'Get rid of corruption.' Increasing numbers of development writers are recognizing this.[2]

On the other side, however, there is a very real danger of the idolization of the free market.

### Free-market capitalism

Free-market capitalism is the economic system that dominates the Western world and to a greater or lesser extent is aspired to by much of the rest of the world.[3] It grew up in Western Europe partly from the way some people interpreted the Bible's teaching, but that was not its only influence. Its basic beliefs are that economic life prospers most when people are as free as possible to pursue their own interests. It is claimed that the markets enable people to exchange their products and services for money, which they in turn can use to buy products and services, with the result that everyone helps each other (without meaning to).

Since the credit crunch and economic crisis of 2007–9 (or longer perhaps), free-market capitalism has been under attack. Some see the whole system as discredited. Others would argue simply that it got out of control in key areas.

On the whole I see many benefits in free-market capitalism. I certainly see the need in a poor country like Sierra Leone (which I know slightly) for wealth creators as much as any other kind of professional. However, I am deeply suspicious of the ways in which free markets become idols and capitalism becomes idolatrous. Far too much faith is placed in them. People make economics their master, not their servant. We know the price of everything but the value of nothing when we swallow capitalism whole.

Above all, capitalism unrestrained by Christian values becomes an idolatrous system in which more is never enough, and contentment is a threat to economic growth which depends on people wanting more and more. So David Wells writes, 'In the rough and tumble scramble for success, our markets are flooded with far more goods, far more choices than we actually need.' He goes on graphically:

The mountainous garbage heaps every city creates, the numerous used car lots, the garage sales, and the storage lockers all tell the

story of use but they tell us the story of desire too. Desire today
is the only norm and this is another indication of the way in
which our modernized world has brought us to a place which,
at a practical level, is godless.[4]

### Barack Messiah Obama

One person who has put hope back into politics is President
Barack Obama. His story is spectacular. His humanity and
ability inspire confidence. He is a great example of political
idolatry. For even a clearly thoughtful and intelligent man
like Barack Obama failed to moderate the expectations
his candidacy generated in 2008 in the USA. One restrained
and insightful commentator remarked on the eve of the
election:

> Expectations for Mr Obama around the world have moved from
> the vocabulary of politics into magic. To hear some claims that
> this is a giant step for mankind you would think that people had
> found a universal saviour.[5]

Sounds like idolatry to me: ascribing to a human being what
is only true of God himself.

Even in cynical Britain we are not exempt from the expectations which political campaigning can generate. Tony Blair's
election campaign in 1997 bopped to the sounds of a hit song
called 'Things Can Only Get Better'. He could hardly complain
when he disappointed everyone! It is perhaps a little mis-
chievous to point out that the song was by a group called
D:Ream. Of course it was a dream, an illusion.

So here are two potential idols: cynicism and excessive
expectation – either in single issues or special leaders. Which
do you tend towards?

Here is another: nationalism.

## National idols

I recently went back to my old school for a reunion. It began with a service in the school chapel which I found rather helpful, but there was one bit when I felt a little uneasy. We were to sing 'I Vow To Thee My Country'. Princess Diana and Prince Charles had it at their wedding. Set to a great tune from *The Planets* by Gustav Holst, it always went down a storm in chapel. As it did this time. But I was uneasy. The first verse is a promise of devotion to one's country:

> I vow to thee, my country, all earthly things above,
> Entire and whole and perfect, the service of my love;
> The love that asks no question, the love that stands the test,
> That lays upon the altar the dearest and the best;
> The love that never falters, the love that pays the price,
> The love that makes undaunted the final sacrifice.

Excuse me, but after the Nuremberg trials where Nazi war criminals argued that they were simply following orders, don't those words sound rather chilling? They could almost have been written as a marching song for the SS, or the Serbian and Croat ethnic cleansing squads of the 1990s, or indeed the British soldiers who signed up for the Boer War when concentration camps were first invented out of a *British* officer's diabolical imagination.

For millions of people around the world, their country is an idol. We may not be proto-fascists, but an idolatry of nation is a real danger.

One writer suggests: 'If a national flag is honoured as the expression of what gives life ultimate meaning, it can become a symbol of idolatry.'[6] That may be worth pondering if your country is one that invests a huge significance in its flag. Why does it do that? Christians need to be careful that a right honouring of their country doesn't become national idolatry.

> Karl Barth is a controversial figure in theology, but he was undoubtedly a penetrating thinker and a very brave man. In the 1930s, when many German Christians were capitulating to Nazism, he saw that fascism was a false religion and that Nazism was idolatrous, and he said so. Publicly. He published articles and in 1933 gave a public lecture about the First Commandment, challenging the basis of Nazism. In the end he lost his job and was expelled for his beliefs.[7]

Nationalism is closely linked to national security and there too lies a potential idol.

### The idol of security and military spending

Here is a powerful statement of the danger of idolizing national security:

> There is no way in which a country can satisfy the craving for absolute security – but it can easily bankrupt itself morally and economically in attempting to reach that goal through arms alone.[8]

Who do you think wrote that? Some left-leaning journalist with no military knowledge or experience? Perhaps an idealistic pastor pontificating on matters beyond his competence (not that pastors ever do that)?

Actually, the man who wrote those words was Dwight Eisenhower, Supreme Commander of the Allied Forces in Western Europe, 1944–5, and President of the USA during the Cold War, 1953–61. What is so interesting is his addition of the word 'morally' to his warning about the ease with which a security-obsessed nation can bankrupt itself economically.

## 9/11 and Iraq

International terrorism, whether or not sponsored by 'rogue states', has become a top priority for Western governments. The events of 9/11 with their parallel attacks in other countries – Bali, Spain, the UK – have shown that the threat is real. But the responses to that threat have often revealed an obsession with security that is simply unrealistic.

## WMD?

The invasion of Iraq by American and British forces in 2003 was based on the explicit evocation of fears for each country's security. It was argued that the existence of weapons of mass destruction and connections between Saddam Hussein's regime and Islamic terrorist groups justified the invasion. Both these assumptions were subsequently revealed to be false. It has been startling to discover the degree to which those responsible for assessing intelligence were disposed to believe the worst and to make the evidence fit the case. It is hard to avoid the impression that popular fears about national security were being played upon to effect the change of a hateful but non-threatening regime.

## Detention and torture

I wasn't convinced that the invasion of Iraq was either just or wise, and preached accordingly on the Sunday before it began.[9] The six years since then have shown that we do face a real threat from terrorism, but that governments are also very prone to overreact, for instance in the British government's attempts to extend detention without trial for terrorist suspects to an unbelievable ninety days, or in the sickening use of torture in the USA's detention centre at Guantanamo Bay. It seems to me that security has become an idol and that the British and American governments have suffered a catastrophic flight of moral capital from their excessive devotion to it (as well as directly causing the deaths of tens of thousands of ordinary Iraqi people).

As British prime minister Stanley Baldwin said in 1932, 'The bomber will always get through.' He was talking about bombs dropped from aircraft, but the same is true of terrorist attacks. Of course governments must take proper precautions against real threats. That is their job (see Romans 13). But we must also beware of them hyping up the threat and imposing illiberal and excessive regulations on us in the name of an unreachable idol of total security.

### Democracy and 'idolatory'

Worship of the Conservative Party in the UK is called 'idolatory'.[10] Sometimes a political movement has noble ideals and understandably inspires a fierce loyalty that easily becomes excessive and therefore idolatrous. In similar ways both extreme left- and extreme right-wing politics are affected by this. Even moderate or centrist parties can be too.

Democracy has become such a noble ideal and a powerful cause that it almost cannot be questioned. However, it is often forgotten that it can lead to the tyranny of a majority over a minority, and democracy is only as good as its politicians and the civic society around it. The scandal over excessive expense claims by British MPs has revealed a moral dissonance at the heart of our democracy.[11]

Christians have every reason to prefer almost any democracy to almost every other government in the world. But sometimes, the way the story of humanity is told, it sounds like a simple upward march to the purest and the best. At that moment democracy becomes an idol.

One writer points out the oddness of the claims made for democracy:

> One difficulty of this approach is to match the high moral pretensions of this narrative with the prosaic realities of electoral democracy as we know it. It seems to aim at nothing less than moral regeneration and this is something altogether grander than the humdrum practice of voting in elections. There is something slightly ridiculous about talk of the dignity of human personality which comes to rest in a slip of paper where we set a cross against the name of someone we do not know![12]

### Marx: idol buster and idol maker

Karl Marx famously suggested that in capitalism money becomes an idol.[13] It is hard to disagree. However, for many who read that (and lots of other things he wrote), Marxism itself became an idol, inducing worship, commitment and obsession. Marx himself made the proletariat, the revolutionary working classes, into a kind of messianic community, with a god-like potential.[14] It was like a replacement for the church, but without a Christ.

Throughout the world in the twentieth century, people read Marx and believed him. They invested all their hopes in the revolutionary movements that developed out of his thinking. They were ready to sacrifice, to live and to die for the cause.

The absolutizing of the cause – a naked idolatry – had terrifying consequences. Lenin boasted of being an 'engineer of souls' who was able to construct a new 'socialist humanity'. The 'end-result of the Bolshevik experiment was mass murder and broken lives on an unprecedented scale. The scale of death in Soviet Russia was rivalled only in Maoist China, another progressive regime.'[15] Since the fall of Eastern bloc communism, those hopes look pretty empty. But the history of Marxism in the twentieth century shows how a political ideal can become an idol.

## Ideas becoming idols: ideology as idolatry

Ideologies are idols with five extra letters. Not that this proves much, but I thought you would like me to point out the obvious. A better definition of ideology is that it is a belief that gains power and demands commitment in society. An example would be some of the political idols we have already considered: both communism and democracy can be ideologies. But ideology isn't purely political. As we will see, it can apply to many areas of human activity. What makes something an ideology is that it tends to be worked out by some apparently rational scheme and to offer some kind of meaning for life or salvation from life's pits.

I can't improve on David Wells's description:

Ideologies . . . are worldviews with an attitude. The intent of every ideology is to *control*. With the passage of time . . . they tend to become simplistic. They find acceptance because they tap into our need . . . 'to believe in single-stroke, cure-all solutions'.

Because they leave only one way out, they become coercive. At the same time, ideologies create a sense of inevitability about themselves. They produce passivity in people because what is inevitable cannot be resisted. And they breed intolerance of those who might be opposed to their understanding of life or might raise questions about it.[16]

### Liberal hu . . . ?

Sometimes it takes a non-Christian to point out that an ideology is an idol. In our age one of the dominant idea systems is liberal humanism. It has a high view of humanity and tolerance. It has been perhaps the reigning intellectual system for most thinking people since Christianity seemed to lose its intellectual credibility. Many who would disdain worshipping cars or careers put all their faith in this ideology. But this is how one non-Christian philosopher describes it:

> Liberal humanism is itself very obviously a religion – a shoddy replica of Christian faith markedly more irrational than the original article and in recent times more harmful.[17]

The same is true of every belief system developed inside and outside of academic circles.

### Darwin the divine

It may be evolution which is inflated from being a generally accepted scientific theory[18] into a total explanation of our humanity, in exclusion of God. It may be cosmology which some attempt to use to rule out the 'need' for God. It may be postmodernism, with its commendable suspicion of the abuse of power, especially in ideology, but which ends up playing its own power games with ideas and texts that produce a new kind of 'strange worship' and dethrone the living God.

An early variety of postmodernism was nihilism – a belief in nothing! No values or truth or meaning. One man who held to it and defended it vociferously was an American philosopher called Jacob Budziszewski. Later

> he became a Christian and admitted what lay behind his
> old commitments: 'The main reason I was a nihilist, the
> reason that tied all these other reasons together, was
> sheer, mulish pride. I didn't want God to be God; I
> wanted J. Budziszewski to be God. I see that now. But
> I didn't see that then.'[19]

Every new current in academia is somewhere affected, even
infected, with idolatrous tendencies. It must be: it is a human
product and our hearts are incurable idol factories, as we have
seen. Students who want to bring every part of their lives
under the lordship of Christ need to work at idol detection in
their lecturers and reading.

## Cultural idols

What is your cultural experience of choice? Music, painting,
sculpture, plays, novels, stories, opera, string quartets, ballet?
Beethoven, Monet, Henry James? The Royal Opera House,
Radio 3, the National Gallery, the Oxford Literary Festival,
the *South Bank Show*? How important is it to you? Is it a gift
from God or an idol to take his place?

### Christ or culture?

I feel particularly strongly about this because I was so affected
by it as a teenager. I was insufferably idealistic and experienced
a two-way pull between Christianity and culture.

At one point I had to write an essay on a novel by D. H.
Lawrence which included some rather beautiful passages
describing spring in New Mexico. I praised the prose and, in
an attempt to show how much it had affected me (!) and
therefore how beautiful it was, I said that it was almost enough
to make me stop being a Christian. Yes, I too think this is

simultaneously pretentious in the extreme and really rather odd. But that is what I wrote.

The teacher responded wisely in the margin that those two didn't have to be alternatives. He was right, though I fear for many, including perhaps even for him, they are. Culture replaces God and is worshipped in the concert halls, libraries and art galleries of the world.

### Beauty as truth?

Beauty for many people *is* truth.[20] If there is any truth, it lies in beauty. Sometimes this comes with huge moral values and expectations, as in the approach of a Cambridge English academic called F. R. Leavis, who died in 1978. He elevated English literature[21] to the level of a religion, believing that it had the moral force to change people for the better. That is idolatry: that is what I was indulging when I wrote that essay.

Creativity and the arts are God-given and biblically endorsed. However, they are also potential idols. Some of us have to watch ourselves carefully here. Do we think ourselves better than others because we listen to Radio 4 rather than Radio 1, or prefer jazz to rap?

Equally, others may be affected by pop culture. Just how important is it to you to have the 'right' ringtone downloaded on your mobile? Is that soap opera which you record when you are on holiday just a bit of innocent escapism, or is it a parallel life that is becoming more real to you than your actual one? What happens when you switch your iPod off for ten minutes and pay attention to what is around you? Is it helping you to be more tuned in to real people? Or is it making you indifferent to them? Remember, we become like what we worship.

## For discussion or personal reflection
Read Colossians 2:6–8.

1. What is Paul glad to see in his first readers?
2. What does he want to guard against?
3. Why does he call the ideas he is concerned about 'hollow' and 'deceptive'? What does that remind you of as we look at the effect that idols have on us?
4. Think about some contemporary idols that are relevant to you. What is their attraction? How are they ultimately empty? What difference should this make to the way you engage with others who are affected by them?

PART TWO

WHAT'S THE BIG PROBLEM?

We have run some diagnostic tests and seen some idols hiding in our hearts which we may have been only half-aware of. We have looked at a sampling of specific idols. Now comes the time to hear a bit more of what God says about idolatry.

# PART TWO

## 9. STRANGE WORSHIP, GLORY SWAPPING

### Strange worship

Let me offer a very simple definition of idolatry. It is 'strange worship'.[1] 'Strange' doesn't normally mean good. It means odd, illogical, puzzling, perplexing, bizarre, outlandish, eccentric, peculiar, weird.[2] We don't do strange things, not usually. Not if it's important. We might try a new and rather odd way of cooking a chicken from a celebrity chef – but probably not for guests before we've tried it ourselves first. We certainly don't base our lives on strange ways of living. That would be very, er, strange! But the Bible says that we do indulge in strange worship – otherwise known as idolatry. Here's the Bible's story of when God revealed that strange worship was wrong. In Exodus God explains it to us.

### Exodus: the great escape

You've escaped. The hated gang-masters have been left far behind. At last you can breastfeed your precious baby son without the risk of the secret police banging on the door, snatching him from your arms and throwing him to the crocodiles. After years of making bricks, you are now making tracks. You are going home – a home you've never been to. But you've heard the stories, and the promises.

### The First Commandment

The sprawling column of men, women and children has taken

a pretty odd route through the desert. Now you are all camped at the bottom of a large rocky mountain. Your leader has gone up into the clouds. It's dark. An earthquake shakes the ground. Red lava flies into the air. Children are crying. An eerie sense of an extraordinary power sends a shiver down your spine. The leader reappears with a couple of rough blocks of stone. People cluster round and he begins to read:

> I am the LORD your God, who brought you out of Egypt, out of the land of slavery.
> You shall have no other gods before me.
> You shall not make for yourself an idol in the form of anything in heaven above or on the earth beneath or in the waters below.
> You shall not bow down to them or worship them; for I, the LORD your God, am a jealous God . . .
> (Exodus 20:2–5 NIV)

You pause, stunned. Then you start to realize what he is saying:

- You are to have only one God, the true God who has rescued you.
- You are not to make images of physical things to worship.
- You have to realize that this is because God is jealous.[3]

### Egyptian gods

You think back to Egypt, with its great cities and powerful imperial civilization. The king, Pharaoh, was known as the Sun-God. The neighbours prayed to goat idols. Your sister put her faith in the bull god to protect her son from the soldiers. You had wondered about praying to the god of the Nile to get you out. Somehow the religion of Jacob and Joseph got a bit confused in Egypt. After all, their god didn't seem to be up to

## But they're all doing it!

### Idolatry in the Ancient Near East

Ancient Near Eastern religion was generally based on idol worship. People believed in gods who could affect their lives: one would give rain if he was feeling pleased with you; another was thought to be a specialist in human fertility. Each tribe or nation had their own special gods who were committed to them. And they all made statues of them. It's easy for us twenty-first-century people to mock them. We are so sophisticated: we know that the planets don't influence our lives . . . Oops: lots of us read our horoscopes, including, it is alleged, Nancy Reagan, wife of one-time US president Ronald Reagan. The second most powerful man in the White House at the time, chief of staff Donald Regan, asserted in his auto-biography that 'virtually every major move and decision the Reagans made during my time as White House Chief of Staff was cleared in advance with a woman in San Francisco who drew up horoscopes to make certain that the planets were in favourable alignment for the enterprise'.[5] Princess Diana was another public figure alleged to have consulted horoscope readers.[6]

### Are idols real?

The people probably thought that the idols were representations of real spiritual entities, 'living feeling beings in which a deity was actually present'.[7] Some were given two meals a day, washed, dressed, and had cosmetics applied (yes, honestly).[8] The statue wasn't the god, but the god was in the statue.[9] So sacrifices were offered to them in the hope of persuading them to bring rain or fertility or success in battle. People invested their hopes and security in idols. They tried to bribe or please or manipulate the idol-deity to favour them. Idol worship was about identity, security, comfort and hope. But it was 'strange worship', because the idols were so inferior to the one true God. Again, we are too sophisticated for all this. Or are we? I am not so sure . . .

much, so why not try some others?[4] Now it is clear who you should worship: the one true God.

The issue of idolatry is not a trivial one. It is right at the heart of what God wants from us. Essentially it is about a choice: do we worship God or not? Do we put something else 'before' him?

### A singular devotion

The true God, the God who rescued the people from Egypt, demanded that his people worship him exclusively. He deserved their total obedience and exclusive worship because he was their identity, their comfort, their security and hope. He deserved it anyway – not just because of what he had done, but because of who he was:

> Ascribe to the LORD the glory due to his name;
>     bring an offering and come into his courts.
> Worship the LORD in the splendour of his holiness;
>     tremble before him, all the earth.
> (Psalm 96:8–9)

God deserves worship: he is incomparable. There is no-one like him. How can something made by human hands possibly compete?

Look at Isaiah 40:12–26. Isaiah mocks people who carve and worship idols, because it is simply so irrational. There is just no comparison between their statues and God. As I type away, changing odd bits of this chapter, I can see the lower slopes of Cadair Idris, one of the tallest mountains in Wales at 893 metres high. It is a great mountain and I love it. So vast, such sheer walls of rock. I couldn't begin to calculate how much it weighs. God not only knows its weight to the nearest gram, he could lift it up and put it in a pair of scales with a flick of his little finger. Isaiah says in effect, 'Show me the idol that could do that!'

### Dumb and inert

Jeremiah compares idols to scarecrows in melon patches (Jeremiah 10:5), made by people, unable to speak, needing to be carried around. They can do neither harm nor good (except when we choose to prefer them to God). In contrast, God is 'the living God'. It's not complicated. Idols are dead: he is alive. He is eternal. He has no beginning and no end. Idols start life in a workshop and finish it on a rubbish tip or in a museum. He made everything: what idol ever made anything? They have to be made themselves (Jeremiah 10:9). It's daft! 'For man to make god is to turn the universe upside down.'[10]

This is just one of many examples in the Old Testament of the sheer irrational strangeness of worshipping idols. What do you worship? What have you put in God's place? It seems so normal and natural, but in fact it is *strange* . . .

The Bible gives us another way of thinking about idolatry: as a crazy, self-harming kind of swap.

## The glory swap

When my son was in Year 2 at his primary school, a craze caught on. It was for 'Pokemon' cards. If you have never heard of them, count yourself fortunate. Pokemon is a kind of card game. Each card shows a Pokemon character: many of them are kinds of made-up animal with different powers. My son and his friends hardly bothered with the game: they simply bought and swapped the cards. Some cards were much rarer than others. I suspect that the manufacturers deliberately created shortages of some of them to drive up the value.[11] When my son came home from school, I used to ask him if he had done any swaps that day. He would always be able to tell me if he had and if they had been 'good swaps' or not.

### The great god swap

Jeremiah uses the language of swapping to express the appalling self-destructive tragedy of idolatry among God's people in his day:

> Has a nation ever changed its gods?
>    (Yet they are not gods at all.)
> But my people have exchanged their Glory
>    for worthless idols.
> (Jeremiah 2:11 NIV)

Generally, people stick with their gods, says Jeremiah. Even when they aren't gods at all. There is a misplaced but real loyalty there. Not in Israel. They are fickle. They change gods like some people change cars. Or kitchens. Or Pokemon cards. And it is a terrible, insane, delusional exchange. In Year 2 playground language, it's a 'rubbish swap'.

Notice how Jeremiah[12] describes the process as 'exchang[ing] their Glory for worthless idols'. There is a great and terrible 'swap' going on – changing glory for something rubbish.

### The privilege of glory

Glory was very important to Israel. The glory of God was right at the centre of God's work in Israel. In Exodus, when the tabernacle was completed, the glory of the Lord filled it (Exodus 40:34–35). Years later, when Solomon completed the temple, again the glory of the Lord filled it (2 Chronicles 7:1).

### Glorious light

The glory referred to the shining bright presence of God. Think of the very brightest light you can imagine, in a cloud of spectacular brightness. The cloud of God's glory shines with the infinite beauty, power, goodness and truth of God himself in all his immensity, infinity and eternity. And it was there in Israel: their privilege, their joy, their responsibility.

### The mad swap

Jeremiah says, 'But my people have exchanged their Glory for worthless idols.' It was their glory, but they traded it away. It's the same for us. We were made to be the image of God, to give him glory, to enjoy his glory and to reflect his glory. In that sense our glory – our greatest privilege, the great goal of our lives, what makes us shine – is his glory: seen, enjoyed and reflected. And we give it away in a terrible swap. We can understand it like this:

1. It means exchanging the worship of the glorious God for the worship of an inglorious idol with no glory to it at all. That's like planting a stinging nettle in the middle of your lawn, instead of a rose bush. Stupid.
2. It means exchanging being close to the acts and presence of God (which have revealed his glory) for being close to an idol which has no power and no living

presence. That's like giving up a meal out with your best friend for a date with a tailor's mannequin. Dumb.

3. It means exchanging the glory of God reflected in our character for the inglorious characteristics of an idol, which would be reflected in our character instead. That's like taking skiing lessons from your Dutch friend who has never left Holland, rather than from the world downhill champion. Mad.[13]

'Exchanging your glory' means giving away your greatest privileges and your most important duties. Madness.

Jean had been brought up in a Christian family and had been baptized at the age of eleven in a wonderful service at church. At university she longed for a Christian boyfriend, but no-one asked her out. Half-way through her accountancy training she met this lovely guy, Scott, in a firm she was auditing. He was passionate about fair trade, full of fun – and he liked the same music. Just the sort of guy she'd like to spend her life with. No, he wasn't a Christian, but he encouraged her to be active in church and he wasn't that far off, she told herself. When he asked her to marry him, she blinked for a moment and said, 'I'd love to.' The marriage worked well, but when the kids came along, weekends and evenings got so full and it was hard to go to church on her own. Eventually she stopped going altogether. Life was full and fulfilling, but when they went back to church for a friend's wedding, she heard a familiar hymn and a great sense of loss grabbed her stomach.

### The glory swap in Romans
Paul picks up Jeremiah's ideas and, interestingly, his exact

words in his letter to the Romans. In chapter 1, he explains
the mess humanity has made of itself like this:

> Although they knew God, they neither glorified him as God nor
> gave thanks to him, but their thinking became futile and their
> foolish hearts were darkened. Although they claimed to be wise,
> they became fools and exchanged the glory of the immortal God
> for images made to look like mortal human beings and birds and
> animals and reptiles.
> (Romans 1:21–23)

Do you see the same words? 'They exchanged the glory of
the immortal God for images . . . ' 'Images' means idols –
visual representations of natural things like people and animals
– to worship.

### It's our story

Paul is telling a story. It takes us right back to Adam and Eve.
It is the story of Israel and the story of the whole human race.
We were made to see, enjoy and reflect the glory of God. Back
in the beginning, men and women were made to be the 'image
and likeness' of God (Genesis 1:26).[14] They had no need to
make images of God to worship: they were to reflect God to
each other and worship him alone in lives of service and
trust.[15] That was their glory. But they did a terrible swap: they
wanted to become like God and to steal his glory; they put
other things in God's place and made them their glory instead.

### It's your story

That pattern is true for every single person. Including you.
Strange worship leads us into a diabolically stupid swap – glory
for shame. And so we 'fall short of the glory of God' and
deserve to be separated from it in hell (Romans 3:23).

*It's your life*

Idol worship is one way of looking at every kind of sin we commit. Sin is not simply breaking a rule (though it is that), or hurting someone (though it does). It is more than transgressing a commandment. It is always about our relationship with the God who loves us and made us; and his right to our gratitude, love and worship. It is about putting something or someone in his rightful place and worshipping that idol instead.

> Idolatry takes many forms but what is common to them all is setting our hearts on something less than God . . . taking that to be God which is not God . . . mistaking some fact or thing or nation or person or dream or possession or ideal for our heart's need and the mystery that moves the sun and other stars.[16]

## For discussion or personal reflection

Read Isaiah 40:12–31.

1. List as many reasons from the passage as you can for why idol worship is 'strange'.
2. How does this impact the original readers' feeling that God had forgotten them (vv. 27–30)?
3. What is the great encouragement for people who will trust God?
4. How have you become deflected from true worship into strange worship? What effect has it had on your life?
5. Write out in your own words why it is stupid for you to trust idols rather than the God who can do what is promised at the end of the chapter.

## Blood on the tracks

Breaking up is almost inevitably heartbreaking for someone. Bob Dylan's album *Blood on the Tracks* was recorded after his divorce. The raw title says it all. Apparently someone told the Great Poet[1] that they had enjoyed the album. 'How can anyone enjoy that kind of pain?' he is supposed to have replied (though the divorce was more his fault than hers).[2]

Alanis Morissette's album *Jagged Little Pill* sounds like one long defiant cry of pain from an experience like that. She is at her shrillest in a no-holds-barred song called 'You Oughta Know', in which she shrieks out her anger at the boyfriend who left her for another girl and the 'mess you left behind'.

## Jilted Jehovah

Being jilted hurts. It is one of the deepest, rawest, most heart-breaking emotions we feel. Early in his book, Jeremiah calls Israel to account for jilting God. Their relationship with him is so close and committed it's like a marriage. And they jilt him. Jeremiah transmits to us the heart cry of a jilted God. When we worship idols, we hurt God as though we've jilted him.

Jeremiah 2 shows jilted Jehovah crying over his people out of love for them. Trying to explain to them how foolish they have been. Warning them of the consequences they are bringing on themselves. Trying to woo them back, so that they will love *him* again. Superficially his song has some similarities to Alanis Morissette's outburst, but ultimately it is, of course, very different. Her song is narcissistic. It is about her and her pain. It's about making him feel bad. It's about getting mad and getting even. God's song is very different.

It is a powerful story that shows us how God feels when we don't put him first. It exposes our spiritual unfaithfulness not just as wicked and offensive to God, but as unproductive and self-destructive. As we trace it, think of your own relationship with Almighty God.

### First love

God looks back sadly:

> I remember the devotion of your youth,
>     how as a bride you loved me
> and followed me through the wilderness,
>     through a land not sown.
> (Jeremiah 2:2)

It had all started so well. God looks back to the early days, centuries before, when he had rescued the people from Egypt. We know from Exodus and Numbers that even then they had their moments. But here he can compare it to the first flush of new love – like so many of us in the first stages of Christian life. But then things went sour.

### What on earth went wrong?

> I brought you into a fertile land
>     to eat its fruit and rich produce.
> But you came and defiled my land
>     and made my inheritance detestable.
> (Jeremiah 2:7)

What possible complaint could they have? He had taken care
of all their needs. He gave them fertile land. But they spoil it
– like moving into a nice house and then trashing it. How?
One word sums it up: *idols*. They have preferred idols and run
after them like a sexually desperate animal:

> Long ago you broke off your yoke
>     and tore off your bonds;
>         you said, 'I will not serve you!'
> Indeed, on every high hill
>     and under every spreading tree
>         you lay down as a prostitute.
> (Jeremiah 2:20)

> See how you behaved in the valley;
>     consider what you have done.
> You are a swift she-camel
>     running here and there,
> a wild donkey accustomed to the desert,
>     sniffing the wind in her craving –
>         in her heat who can restrain her?
> Any males that pursue her need not tire
>         themselves;
>     at mating time they will find her.
> Do not run until your feet are bare
>     and your throat is dry.
> But you said, 'It's no use!
>     I love foreign gods,
>     and I must go after them.'
> (Jeremiah 2:23–25)

God has been betrayed. He speaks the sad and angry words
of a jilted husband. It is worth pondering this, because so often

we think of our sin as just breaking rules. In addition it is a personal betrayal. We hurt God.

## The jealous God

That is the first thing our idolatry does – it betrays and saddens God. It is important to state that upfront. That is what is most offensive about idolatry: what it does to God. Remember the way he describes it:

> You shall have no other gods before me.
>     You shall not make for yourself an idol . . . You shall not bow down to them or worship them; *for I, the LORD your God, am a jealous God.*
> (Exodus 20:3–5 NIV, emphasis mine)

He is a jealous God. Divine jealousy may well be the 'basic element of the whole Old Testament idea of God'.[3] God will not be spurned, or cheated on. When people try to jilt God, he reacts with a pure jealousy which reveals just how much he cares for us and how committed he is to being glorified in us through our delight in him.[4] Later he even says to Moses that his name is Jealous (Exodus 34:14).

### When jealousy is OK

We think of jealousy as a negative thing, but it isn't necessarily so. An English radio personality who used to be a member of the UK parliament was known for having an open marriage. He admitted as much in his autobiography. He and his wife agreed that they could sleep with other people and neither would mind. Does that sound enlightened . . . or just sad? Surely every human instinct shouts at us that he ought to be jealous when his wife goes home with another man.

Certainly *God* is jealous for his people's hearts and faithfulness. But they repeatedly betrayed him. Jeremiah goes on to throw up his hands in horror at the unfaithfulness of both Israel and Judah:

'But like a woman unfaithful to her husband,
so you, house of Israel, have been unfaithful to me,'
    declares the LORD.
(Jeremiah 3:20)

In the New Testament there is a subtle reminder that God hasn't changed. In 1 Corinthians 10 Paul urges the readers in first-century Corinth to avoid joining in with the eating that went with idol worship in the temples there. To ram his point home, he asks them, 'Are we trying to arouse the Lord's jealousy?' (1 Corinthians 10:22).

Think about that for a moment. God longs for your heart to be devoted to him. He is jealous about your unfaithfulness. His response to your trusting other things more than him is like that of a betrayed husband.

## Idols produce tears

When I was at school, 'crybaby bunting' was just about the worst playground insult. To be a crybaby is to be a worm. Generations have grown up being told, 'Big boys don't cry.' There is a character in Rossini's opera *The Barber of Seville* who says, 'I make myself laugh at everything for fear of having to weep at it.' But sometimes weeping is the right thing to do. No-one laughed when the earthquake hit Kashmir in 2005. There are precious few comedy gags about tsunamis. Only tears will do.

Jeremiah has been nicknamed the 'weeping prophet'. He weeps more than anyone else in the Bible. Tears were the only possible reaction to what he saw and lived through.

Once my family was talking about crying at supper. My younger daughter (then aged six) said something that struck us: 'Crying is having sadness running down your face.' Jeremiah saw the idolatry of his people and sadness ran down his face:

> Since my people are crushed, I am crushed;
> I mourn, and horror grips me.
> (Jeremiah 8:21)

> Oh, that my head were a spring of water
>     and my eyes a fountain of tears!
> I would weep day and night
>     for the slain of my people.
> (Jeremiah 9:1)

'Lord, make my eyes like a power shower. Turn me into Niagara Falls.' He needs a huge volume of water to express his horror. Ordinary tears would run too slowly and run out too quickly.

### Who's crying?

We might be tempted to say that this is just dismal old Jeremiah, the weeping prophet. Perhaps he had epiphora, a medical condition which means your tears flow constantly.[5] Or maybe he was just a bit oversensitive.

It is not always clear who is speaking. It looks as if it's Jeremiah from verse 21 onwards. But many commentators point to the end of verse 3 and argue that we can't be sure where Jeremiah stops and God starts. The same uncertainty is present in 9:7–11 as well. Even commentators who resist this reading admit that Jeremiah stands for God here. Jeremiah's tears are an echo of God's tears. As Jeremiah weeps for his people, he expresses the broken heart of God.

### Thank God he's not English

English men are not known for their emotional expressiveness.
Kate Fox, an anthropologist, argues that in spite of this they
do conform to what she calls 'the three emotion rule':

> English males are allowed to express . . . some emotions. Three
> to be precise: surprise, providing it is conveyed by expletives;
> anger, generally communicated in the same manner; and elation/
> triumph which again often involves shouting and swearing. It can
> thus sometimes be rather hard to tell exactly which of the three
> permitted emotions an Englishman is attempting to convey.[6]

God has no such inhibitions. It is part of God's greatness that
he is a passionate God. It is part of his greatness that he
expresses his passion for us to turn back to him. It is perfectly
clear what he is feeling.

### God's feelings

It is a relief to find that God is not at the mercy of his emotions
in the way we are. He has a perfect emotional self-control that
we lack. He is never ambushed or surprised by his emotions
as we are. His emotions never lead him to do things he later
regrets as ours do. But he is still a feeling God, and he feels for
*us*. He has decided to be passionate about us. And so he longs
for us and for what is best for us. He yearns for us to stop
running away from him, to come to our senses and run back
to him.

### God's tears

God weeps over this fallen world. He weeps for its wounds.
He weeps for the judgment that is coming on it. He weeps for
the idolatry that insults him and brings misery on those who
perpetrate it. And so did his Son.

### Jesus' tears

> As [Jesus] approached Jerusalem and saw the city, he wept over it.
> (Luke 19:41)

This is Jesus' Jeremiah moment. He cries over the doomed city. Then he enters the temple and quotes Jeremiah! Commenting on this passage, Tom Wright says:

> Jesus' tears are at the core of the Christian gospel. This is not a moment of regrettable weakness, something a real Messiah ought to have avoided.

He had kept warning his people that unless they repented, judgment would come and the temple would crash to the ground. Jesus' warning message to his people is 'uttered finally through sobs and tears'.

> The terrible judgement that has been pronounced and will be shortly executed proceeds not from a stern and cold justice but from a heart of love that wants the best for and from the people and so must now oppose, with sorrow and tears, the rebellions that had set its own interests and agendas before those of the God who had established them there in the first place.[7]

Let's go back to Jeremiah to see how strongly he reacts:

> 'Be appalled at this, you heavens,
> and shudder with great horror,' declares the LORD.
> (Jeremiah 2:12)

It is so unnatural, so heinous, so terrible that creation should react with horror. It is important for us to realize that the first and chief reason why we should understand and repudiate idolatry is that it is so deeply insulting to Almighty God. If we start with its effect on *us*, we make ourselves the centre of everything: we simply analyse idolatry as a cause of depression or anxiety; we may just read this book as a way of improving ourselves. But that would sell God short.

It is much worse than the source of my own pain: my idolatry sets the stratosphere howling; when I prefer idols to the living God, I send spasms of horror through the galaxy. My drinking from the cisterns of idolatrous sex, idolatrous attitudes to family, idolized careers and accumulated possessions appals the entire universe.

Of course it produces his judgment:

> 'Your wickedness will punish you;
>> your backsliding will rebuke you.
> Consider then and realise
>> how evil and bitter it is for you
> when you forsake the LORD your God
>> and have no awe of me,'
> declares the Lord, the LORD Almighty.
> (Jeremiah 2:19)

## For discussion or personal reflection
Read Exodus 20:3–5.

1. What is your first reaction to reading that our God is a 'jealous' God?
2. Discuss why God's jealousy is actually a positive and holy thing.
3. What sorts of things is God jealous of in our lives?
4. How does thinking about that affect you?

Read Luke 19:41; Jeremiah 8:21; 9:1.

1. What do these passages teach us about God?
2. What difference does that make to our view of him?
3. Imagine if you took these passages seriously: how
   would your life be different?

Spend some time praising God for what you have learned
about him.

## 11. WHAT IDOLS DO TO US

### Walking holidays in the desert

Depending on your age, imagine that you have joined a gap year/18–30s/family adventure/Christian singles/Saga Holidays walking tour in a hot country.[1] Syria, perhaps, or Jordan. There are Crusader castles and deep wadis and camels and hills and dust. Lots of dust. The path is dusty. The rocks are dusty. The whole landscape feels dusty. You look at your companions. A thin layer of white dust covers each of them. It is like a hike with ghosts. Shoulders are slumping; dragging your legs forward is more and more of an effort. And your throat is parched. The end of the day is approaching. The heat has been extreme. Your water has just about run out.

#### Dry as dust

A village is spotted about half a mile off. Suddenly there's a spring in everyone's step. 'They must have water here.' 'Of course they do.' 'There's probably a spring.' The guide looks confused. 'That village has moved. It used to be another three miles that way,' he says, as he points over a low ridge that right now looks like Mount Everest. But you don't care: it's three miles nearer – great!

#### Grotty water

The village elders come out to meet you. 'Welcome!' they say. 'Come inside and have a drink.' In their mud houses, they present you with a small clay cup, half full of water. At least you suppose it must be water. But it is slightly brown looking and, as you peer more closely, you see there are little squiggly things squiggling around in it.

'Thanks,' you mumble croakily as you gulp it down. It tastes awful.

'We can't offer you any more,' says the woman apologetically. 'The container doesn't hold the rain very well and it's empty. Sorry.' That gets you off the hook: you'd been trying to work out whether to accept more of this disgusting stuff or risk feeling parched all evening.

### What an odd lot!

Your guide joins the group. 'I thought this village used to be further down the road,' he says, 'next to the spring.'

'We moved,' they reply.

'Why?'

'We didn't like the spring. We prefer these big underground storage cisterns.'

'But the water runs out of them and anyway, it's not fresh,' says the guide.

They shrug their shoulders and say nothing. And you look at the squiggly things and the mud and think they must be mad.

In Jeremiah 2, the prophet uses precisely this image to show the people of Israel what idol worship does to them and how lunatic it is.

My people have committed two sins:
They have forsaken me,
    the spring of living water,
and have dug their own cisterns,
    broken cisterns that cannot hold water.
(Jeremiah 2:13)

Cisterns were large, pear-shaped underground holes that you could dig if you didn't have a spring. Rainwater would collect in them. But the clay linings often cracked, so the water seeped away. Even if some stayed at the bottom, it was often brackish and unpleasant, full of algae and those funny little squiggly things. My dog drinks water like that. Sometimes he spurns the bowl of fresh tap water we put out for him and drinks the horrible greenish sludge that has collected in a flower pot. I wouldn't! I don't think you would either.

Jeremiah uses this picture to expose the appalling, idiotic self-destructiveness of idolatry. One writer has said that 'idolatry is not so much the infraction of a divine command as an act of cosmic insanity'.[2] Idolatry messes us up: 'in the hour of greatest need it utterly fails.'

What does the water from those broken cisterns do to us? To understand its effect properly, we need to go back a little earlier in Jeremiah 2, to verse 5.

## How idols fail us

> This is what the LORD says:
> 'What fault did your ancestors find in me,
>     that they strayed so far from me?
> *They followed worthless idols*
>     *and became worthless themselves.'*
> (Jeremiah 2:5, emphasis mine)

Another version translates the last two lines like this:

> They . . . walked after emptiness and became empty.[3]

### Hollow men and women
Idols do not improve us, they reduce us. They hollow us out.

They leave us less than we were. Less human, less satisfied, less of what we could be and should be. And they do this by making us like themselves.

> The idols of the nations are silver and gold,
>     made by the hands of men.
> They have mouths, but cannot speak,
>     eyes, but they cannot see;
> they have ears, but cannot hear,
>     nor is there breath in their mouths.
> *Those who make them will be like them,*
>     *and so will all who trust in them.*
> (Psalm 135:15–18 NIV, emphasis mine)

### Becoming like them

Greg Beale puts it like this: 'What we revere we resemble.'[4] He's written a whole book showing the connection between idolatry and human degradation. Because idols are deaf and dumb, we lose sensitivity. Because they have no personal substance, we lose human and moral weight when we worship them. Our idols are unreal. They are idle! They can't bear the weight we put on them. Like thin ice, they give way and leave us soaking wet and shivering with cold. Because they have no substance, when we trust them our lives feel unreal, lightweight, shadowy. Our hearts become more hollow and less whole. One writer puts it like this: 'Pursue a bubble and become a bubble.'[5]

### It's no comedy

Isn't that a tragedy? We were made for something far better. Human beings are wired and designed to know God in his glory; to find our greatest hopes and joys in him; to reflect his glory. When our hearts get diverted onto catalogue shopping, or bringing up perfect children, or climbing the greasy pole of a medical career, we degrade ourselves. Something in our humanity shrivels and decays.

> When we forget who God truly is, it is but a short step to
> forgetting who we are and who our neighbour is . . . a
> disintegration and dehumanisation takes place in the aftermath
> of a departure from the Living God.[6]

Hosea describes this hollowing out devastatingly by comparing idol worshippers to four images of lightweight insignificance: morning mist which the sun burns off, dew which is evaporated by elevenses time, corn husks which the wind blows away, and smoke from a fire which blows out through a window (Hosea 13:2–3).

> When I arrived, Chrystal was just sitting down. He was
> smoking a pipe and his expression was not as elated as it
> had been that morning. Even when Brown produced a
> bottle of [wine] Chrystal responded with a smile that
> was a little twisted, a little wan. He was dispirited because
> his triumph like all triumphs had not been as intoxicating
> as he had imagined it.[7]

Let's take one test case. Our culture reveres success when it brings fame. Children long to be pop stars or footballers to achieve those things. We idolize them. Sadly, neither success nor fame necessarily brings satisfaction. Here are four successful people in rare moments of honesty.

### The politician
Jonathan Aitken was at one time a rising star of the 1990s

Conservative government in Britain. All was not well deep down, however. He wrote later:

> In my heart of hearts, I was aware that something was going seriously wrong with my hitherto vaulting ambition and my appetite for power. What that something wrong was, I did not know. All I could tell was that the more my career prospered on the surface, the more my deeper feelings were signalling an emptiness and lack of fulfilment within . . . Gnawing away inside me was a problem I could not describe, except [through] labels such as 'lack of inner peace', 'emptiness of feeling', 'hollowness of spirit', or more simply 'something missing'. It was as though, after spending a lifetime wanting to climb a particular mountain, I had unexpectedly reached the final approach to its summit only to discover that there was nothing there worth the effort of the ascent.[8]

### The Wimbledon winner

Boris Becker, the famous tennis champion, came close to taking his own life while feeling overwhelmed by a sense of emptiness and hopelessness. Successful as he was, something was missing.

> I had won Wimbledon twice, once as the youngest player [ever]. I was rich, I had all the material possessions I needed: money, cars, women, everything . . . I know this is a cliché. It's the old song of the movie and pop stars who commit suicide. They have everything, and yet they are so unhappy . . . I had no inner peace. I was a puppet on a string.[9]

### The writer

Jack Higgins, the highly successful thriller writer, was at the top of his profession. He was asked what he now knew that he would like to have known when he was a boy. It is reported that he replied, 'That when you get to the top, there's nothing there.'[10]

## The actress

Raquel Welch was reckoned one of the great beauties of her day. Her photograph was everywhere. Looking back on the height of her success, she wrote:

> I had acquired everything I wanted, yet I was totally miserable . . . I thought it was very peculiar that I had everything I wanted as a child – wealth, fame, and accomplishment in my career. I had beautiful children and a lifestyle that seemed terrific, yet I was totally and miserably unhappy. I found it very frightening that one could acquire all these things and still be so miserable.[11]

## The hollow people

Idol worship fails to satisfy us and hollows us out as people. It is not just the rich and powerful who find this: we all do. Have you ever felt 'thinner'? Hollowed out? Empty? Not physically, but emotionally and psychologically. The reason is almost certainly something to do with worshipping idols. We think they are real and strong and able to give us something we crave – but we find that in reality they are insubstantial, and worshipping them hollows us out.

It had all started so well. James loved physics: he worked hard at his A levels, got onto the BSc course he applied for and did well enough to enrol for a PhD. It was so exciting to work with one of the leading experts in his field. Longer and longer hours seemed like more and more fun. Unfortunately Alice, his girlfriend, didn't see it the same way. At first she tolerated the weekends in the lab, trying to feel privileged to be going out with such a promising young scientist. Increasingly, though, what worried her was that even when they did get an evening together in the Japanese noodle bar, James seemed different. Eventually she moved to another city, deeply upset at breaking up, but feeling it was the right thing to do. James was a little sad, but perked up at the thought of more time in the lab. Three years later, he suddenly realized he never really went out with anyone, even just socially, and that if he did he wouldn't know what to say to them. 'I feel as though I've become a kind of human computer,' he confided to someone he met on an internet chat room.

## Judgment

The effect of idolatry goes further: it cuts us off from God and exposes us to his judgment. The message of Jeremiah and Isaiah and so many of the prophets was that idolatry had roused God's anger and would bring his judgment on the people. Jesus repeats that message. Repeatedly. Idolatry produces judgment: loss in this life, eternal pain afterwards. God holds us to account for our strange worship and our glory swap. Because of the idolatry of greed, his wrath is coming (Colossians 3:5–6). The sensual sins of sexual immorality and materialistic greed are idols which keep people out of God's new creation (Ephesians 5:5).

### *Not here, thanks!*

Judgment is a difficult subject. I never find it easy to preach – partly because it is unpopular, partly because I know I deserve it too. Judgment is real, but I found these words helpful in working out my posture as I explain it:

The church comes with a judgment upon the modern world, but it is not the kind of judgment which enables the Christian to feel superior; not the kind that makes him say: 'What a ghastly world this is that we Christians have to cope with,' not that at all. The church's judgment upon the modern world is very different. It is properly expressed when we turn to our contemporaries and say: 'Look what we've done, you and I. Luxury here and famine there; juvenile delinquency, prostitution, alcoholism, the revival of slavery, racial discrimination, look what we've done. Look what our human nature produces when it gets a free hand, unrestrained by God. Do you want it like that? Do you like it like that? Is that your idea of a worthwhile world?'[12]

That is helpful, but it does not remove the basic truth: the human race will be held to account for its strange worship and its glory exchange. And the consequences for those not forgiven through Christ will be terrible.

Idolatry brings disappointment and degradation in this life and everlasting destruction[13] in the next. That is what it does to us.

## For discussion or personal reflection
Read Jeremiah 2:1–13.

1. What is the tone of this piece of poetic poetry? What does that tell us?
2. Look again at verse 5. How does this explain your own feelings of hollowness?
3. 'We become like what we worship.' How does this connect with your life?
4. Look again at verse 13. What are the two sins that Israel has committed?

5. Why is it ludicrous to prefer cistern water to spring water? How is the image intended to affect us emotionally? How does it connect with your life?
6. What is God calling you to change in your life?

# PART THREE

# IDOL BUSTING

It is time now to think about how we can find freedom from our idols.

By now you will have detected some idols in your life. But insight alone butters no parsnips, as Bertie Wooster used to say.[1] We need more than merely to understand our idols: we need to escape from them. The good news – no, the greatest news – is that in Christ that is possible!

I have a cousin who was made redundant, so he set up his own company. It offered to do all sorts of administration bits and pieces for small businesses: red tape, accounts, payroll – all kinds of things. He called his company 'Drudgebuster', as it took away those boring but essential little jobs that people called the 'drudge' of their work.

## Idol busters

The next few chapters are about God's 'idol busters'. We need him and his idol busters, or we have no hope of escape. If you are not a Christian (or if as a Christian you try to escape idols in a sub-Christian way), you may be able to escape one idol and its effects through insight and willpower, but another will replace it.

Only in Christ will you find true freedom (Galatians 5:1). He has done everything necessary, but we have our part too: in this chapter we will be thinking about the importance of repenting of our idolatrous sins, receiving his forgiveness, realizing that we are God's children and living in the power of his Spirit. Think of these as our 'idol busting'.

## A framework

How can we go about idol busting? There are lots of different angles we could take. After all, the whole of the Bible after Genesis 3 is essentially about God busting idols and reclaiming human hearts. There is one great verse in Isaiah that gives us a framework for the next few chapters:

> This is what the Sovereign LORD, the Holy One of Israel, says:
> 'In repentance and rest is your salvation,
>     in quietness and trust is your strength,
>     but you would have none of it.'
> (Isaiah 30:15)

He is responding to Israelite idolaters whose pursuit of foreign gods and strange worship has left them in crisis. They have formed an unholy alliance with Egypt rather than trusting in the Lord's protection. Though challenged, they reject God's messengers with chilling self-deception:

> 'Give us no more visions of what is right!
> Tell us pleasant things,
>     prophesy illusions. . .
> and stop confronting us
>     with the Holy One of Israel!'
> (Isaiah 30:10–11)

God replies that their sin will implode:

> like a high wall, cracked and bulging,
> that collapses suddenly, in an instant.
> (Isaiah 30:13)

But he doesn't leave it there. He shows them a way out: through repentance and rest. It is our way out of the shattered dreams and ingrained habits of our idolatry too. The next few chapters will explore idol busting through repentance and rest.[2]

## Repentance

What is meant by 'repent'? We need to know, because repentance is core for Christians. Jesus summarized the message of the gospel as an announcement of repentance and forgiveness of sins through him (Luke 24:47). Have you repented and put your faith in him? If not, you won't be able to break free from your idols. Even feeling sorry isn't enough. There are two kinds of sorrow about idols.

### The wrong kind

There are wrong kinds of repentance. Paul describes it as 'worldly sorrow' (2 Corinthians 7:10). We are sorrowful in a worldly way when we simply regret what has happened. Like a TV presenter or other public figure who says something horrendously and objectively offensive, but only apologizes for any offence that 'may have been taken'. Or when we are sad at the bad effects our idolatry has had on us, but only sad for ourselves. Sometimes I catch my dog on the first-floor landing of our house, outside the children's bedrooms: he looks sheepish, but he's only sorry he was found out. Worldly sorrow is *self*-centred, not *God*-centred.

### The right kind

Godly sorrow is just that: godly. It is God-centred. It recognizes that above all idolatry is an insult to God. Idolatry causes pain to God. Idolatry robs God of his glory. Idolatry is an appalling act of rebellion against God. Idolatry spurns the love of the wise, kind, loving God whose goodness and beauty are all that we could ever need. It says he's not good enough for us: we need to worship something else to be happy. Godly sorrow leads to repentance for all that.

> Ian let himself down repeatedly: sudden outbursts of temper, failing to stand up for Christian values, passing on sly bits of gossip. It made him feel terrible about himself. He hated it. Each time he was determined to do better. He thought that if he did, he would at last feel OK. It never seemed to work. He wondered why.

### A choice and a process

Repentance means a decision to take the steps needed to change our attitudes and behaviour. It is a single, willing decision, a commitment to change. But it is not a self-confident decision to do better, as if everything can be changed by a single act of will. Our habits are too well grooved, our distorted beliefs too ingrained, our imaginations too deeply confused, for that to work. Repentance is a commitment to a process in which the idol is taken off its pedestal in our hearts, God is worshipped instead, his Holy Spirit is invited to work in our lives, and so our behaviour changes.

### Day by day

Repentance needs to be a habit. A daily habit. This is one of the great insights of an American leader called Jack Miller. He wrote that in the death of Jesus for us, 'God promises to receive contrite sinners on a daily – no, hourly – basis.'[3] Repentance is not a one-off act. It is the shape of our lives. Only through habits of repentance can the idols be dethroned.

Apply this to your idolatry. First, ask yourself these things: Are you consistently repenting of your idolatry? Have you come to a place of 'godly sorrow'? Have you taken the first decisive step of repentance, and started to work on a process of change?

Have you repented of your efforts to improve yourself?[4]

> Jack Miller had a terrible shock one day. In the middle of a mission trip in Mexico, he was about to speak at a conference when his daughter Barbara (aged eighteen) announced to Jack and his wife Rose Marie that she didn't believe in their rules, faith or way of life any more. His wife just shouted at her. Jack listened quietly and said, 'I need to understand God's love in a deeper way.' He spent the next two weeks writing for himself about how God's love has to be experienced through repentance. He had to repent of the ways in which he had failed his daughter. When they went home to Pennsylvania, Jack found he had to keep repenting of those sinful urges to be in control or not to believe God. As his daughter's life deteriorated in shocking ways, he 'kept returning to his need for the presence of the Spirit'. But, he wrote, learning to confess his sins more 'forthrightly' and turning from them 'with deeper hatred for every evil impulse in my heart' gave a 'joy and relief' to his 'struggling soul' which was 'simply beyond words', the 'glory of the cross appeared . . . with transforming and healing power'.[5]

### Repentance brings forgiveness

Salvation comes through faith in Christ. Simply being sorry for a pattern of idolatry is not enough. We need *forgiveness*. We may have hurt ourselves through our idols, but much more important is the fact that we have offended God.

### Death to guilt

Through Christ, we *can* be forgiven. His death guarantees that forgiveness is a constantly available reality. The cross is sufficient for all our sins, past, present and future. It is not as though it is enough for some sins and not for others, like a weedkiller that only deals death blows to the weaker kinds of weed. Christ's death covers every single kind of idolatry, however deep-seated, long-standing or all-pervading it is. It is sufficient for the guilt of every idolatrous thought, attitude, desire, word or act. As we break free from idols, we must do so by exercising faith in Christ, not by thinking for a moment that we can save ourselves. All thoughts of paying God back for the offence we have caused must be thrown in the river of discarded thought to be swept far away downstream.

### Instant, total and free

I like to tell my church that forgiveness is *instant* (we don't have to wait), *total* (it covers everything) and *free* (it is a totally un-earned, undeserved gift). Just think of that for a moment. You heard it when you became a Christian, but perhaps you have forgotten. Forgiveness is instantaneous. There is no delay. It is total. It covers every single sin; the worst of your sins; the ones you can hardly bring to mind and shudder to think of admitting to anyone else; all of them. It is completely free. You contribute nothing. It is not dependent on your work, but on Christ's.

### Peace in our time

Forgiveness has another aspect that is very important as we think of breaking free from idolatry: it means we are at peace with God.

> Therefore, since we have been justified through faith, we have
> peace with God through our Lord Jesus Christ, through whom

we have gained access by faith into this grace in which we now stand.
(Romans 5:1–2)

Idolatry insults God and creates a barrier between us. Forgiveness breaks down the barrier. Even if we are already Christians, love of idols can make a dark cloud pass over the loving sun of God's face. Forgiveness brings us close to God. If we are already Christians, it renews our closeness to him. This is also very important in our battle against idols. The way God deals with them is to woo our hearts to prize, esteem and value him and his promises more.

### Condemnation and idols

At the start of Romans 8 there is a great statement of what follows repentance and faith: 'Therefore, there is now no condemnation for those who are in Christ Jesus' (8:1).

> Steph grew up in a home of rules and criticism. She learned to believe from her parents, but not just in Christ: they taught her to believe in her own worthlessness too. Out every evening in church activities, up every morning for an hour of unsatisfying prayer, never feeling she was good enough – eventually she settled into a deep depression. A friend sent her a card with a verse on it: 'There is now no condemnation for those who are in Christ Jesus.' And she saw where she had been going wrong.

This is highly important. Fear of condemnation is what drives so much idol worship. The deep idol of approval lies behind so many surface idols. We fear what people will think of us and become neurotically anxious about our appearance or our work, making both into little gods.

### Condemning ourselves

What is condemning us? For most of us it is our sin and our consciences. We don't need anyone else to do it. We are accusing ourselves and condemning ourselves again and again. Guilt and shame spoil our walk with the Lord. They hold us back from serving him because we feel too unworthy. They prevent us from properly engaging with the needs of others because we are too preoccupied with ourselves. They make us crabby and critical towards others as we try to deflect attention from ourselves.

We hear the voice in our heads. The video of our lives replays itself. The guilt and shame won't go away. And it eats away at our assurance like acid dripping on metal.

Some of us grew up in homes where we heard charge after charge after charge against us. Some of us seem to be wired to keep bringing charges against ourselves. Some of us constantly fear the charges others bring against us, imagining criticism and accusation constantly even where there is none.

### No condemnation any more

This is our remedy. No condemnation. Not now. Not at the final judgment. And the Lord wants to say to many of us, 'Stop condemning yourself. Stop doing to yourself what your parents or schoolmates or teachers may have done to you. Stop living a life dominated by unresolved guilt.'

'There is now no condemnation for those who are in Christ Jesus' (Romans 8:1). Step out of the shadows of God's love and into the full light. Stand before him confidently. You can raise your head up and meet his gaze. You now live in a 'room called grace',[6] trusting in Christ, sure that you are safe, rejoicing in what God has done for you.

It releases us from one very real kind of idolatry: caring too much what other people think. The Bible sometimes calls it the 'fear of man'. The work of the Holy Spirit is designed to destroy such fear and to replace it with confidence in God as our Father (Romans 8:15).

Fear of people is a crippling experience, whether you are vicar of a parish, leader of the free world or a volunteer in a charity shop. In his brilliant book *When People Are Big and God Is Small*, Ed Welch suggests that 'the answer is straightforward: We must learn to know that our God is more loving and more powerful than we ever imagined.'[7] We might add these words: 'And has pronounced "no condemnation" over us.'

John had a nice group of friends who seemed to let him take the lead: that was the way he liked it. One way or another, he could generally get them to do what he wanted to do, so skilfully (he thought) that no-one really noticed. One day his girlfriend Anna challenged him about it. She pointed out how self-centred it was. He'd apologized to his friends by email and they'd been really nice about it, but the sense of failure lingered. John felt terrible when he went to church that Sunday and it was such a relief to hear the words of the liturgy which he knew so well tripping off the vicar's lips: 'Almighty God, who forgives all who truly repent, have mercy upon us, pardon and deliver us from all our sins.' Afterwards, as the group were planning where to go for a picnic, he found himself apologizing all over again. 'What for?' said Anna. 'We've forgiven you totally – just like God.'

## For discussion or personal reflection

Read 2 Corinthians 7:8–11.

1. What different kinds of sorrow do you have for your
   idols?
2. What would it look like for you to repent properly?
3. What have you repented of recently? Anything specific?
   If there isn't anything specific, what does that say?

Read Romans 8:1.

4. What happens to us if we don't trust that there is 'no
   condemnation' for us any more?

## Adoption

The next stage of idol busting is to realize who we are: children of God, adopted into his own family and made new by his Holy Spirit.

> God sent him to buy freedom for us who were slaves to the law, so that he could adopt us as his very own children. And because we are his children, God has sent the Spirit of his Son into our hearts, prompting us to call out, 'Abba, Father.'
> (Galatians 4:5–6 NLT)

The implications of our spiritual adoption by God are almost too good to be true: 'In adoption, God takes us into his family and fellowship and establishes us as his children and heirs. Closeness, affection and generosity are at the heart of the relationship.'[1]

Adoption is the most wonderful truth about you if you are a Christian.

- It is an unshakable legal truth.[2]

The passage of time will not change it. Your adoption is for ever.

- It is a life-changing relational truth.

Time will not see God's interest in us wobble. The passing of the years will just help us realize how complete his commitment to us is.

- It is a powerful emotional truth.

Time will not reduce its power to thrill us. Instead time will reveal to us just how deeply he loves us and how passionately he cares for us. If you have trusted in Christ, God has become your Father. You have become his child.

### Your true Father

One of your parents may have died when you were quite young. My wife's grandfather was like that. His father was killed in the trenches of the First World War before he was even born. It leaves a lifelong hole.

> You may have grown up with an aching gap in your life. But he knew; he drew you to himself. You have a Father now – you are not cheated.[3]

Perhaps for you the word 'father' doesn't have very good associations. It may be an effort for you to call God 'Father' because of the past.

> God stands in contrast to many earthly parents. They were brutal: he is gentle. They were indifferent, he was committed. They were foolish; he is wise. They were distant: he has no inhibitions. He is the Father you always wanted and you are his wanted and cherished child.[4]

What a powerful truth – about you! Now apply it to your patterns of idolatry. Where are you trying to find comfort, security, affirmation, hope? Turn from those idols and trust in your heavenly Father instead.

### Adoption and identity

One issue I had to work through during my five months off work with clinical depression was where my identity lay. Identity issues are big idols for many of us in ministry. We gain our sense of who we are from our crammed diaries, our important speaking engagements, the positive feedback we get from our sermons or visits. We would never admit it, but deep down we get our sense of well-being, meaning, achievement and perhaps even status with God from our service to him in church. At least I discovered how much I did. I guess it applies equally to other fields of work: status, busyness, achievement – those are the things which define us.

It was really brought home to me a couple of weeks after I had started back at work. The morning service finished and as usual I made my way to the front door of our church building to shake hands with people as they left. As usual my colleague Marvin Wong was standing next to me. After a few people had gone past us both, I became aware of some negative feelings.

People were shaking Marvin's hand and saying, 'Great sermon, Marvin!' or, 'That was so helpful, Marvin.' Or they were asking to see him, so he was getting his diary out of his pocket to make a date.

Then they were going past me, shaking my hand and saying, 'Nice to see you, Julian.' No words of appreciation for what I had done in the service, because I hadn't done anything to be appreciated. No requests to meet, as I wasn't doing any pastoral work at that stage. My diary remained firmly in my pocket. I might as well have left it at home. After this happened a dozen times or so, I began to feel totally useless, like a spare tyre with an unfixed puncture.

I took a moment to think about it and realized that deep down I was building my identity on my ministry and without ministry I was in danger of evaporating away. 'How stupid!' I said to myself. 'I am a child of God. That's where my identity comes from, not whether I have preached a sermon!' I went back to shaking hands and smiling, feeling much better. Another idol had been exposed and the Holy Spirit was helping me dethrone it.

## Repentance brings Spirit renewal

Closely linked to our being made God's children is the work of the Holy Spirit to make us *feel* that we are God's children, to give what the theologians call 'assurance'. One writer who himself has three adopted children observes that 'adopted children need assurance that they belong and a perfect parent will not withhold it'.[5] The Holy Spirit gives that assurance and even prompts us to call God 'Father'.

### Only by the Spirit

The Holy Spirit does more: in his letter to the Galatians Paul shows that the Spirit is absolutely key to a life becoming free from idolatry.[6] We all have this Spirit, because God gave him to us when we believed the gospel (Galatians 3:2). God continues to supply the Spirit to us (3:5) as we keep believing the gospel. It is by living by the Spirit that idolatry is removed from our lives (5:16) and we can grow towards personal and spiritual maturity (3:2). Living by the Spirit means making dependence on him and obedience to him the basic way we try to live the Christian life (3:18). Rules and regulations without dependence on him will tend to turn into idolatrous self-justification. We can unfortunately get out of step with him, so it is vital for us to check whether this has happened. If it has, we need to repent and get back in step.

That was a bit of a heavy paragraph, wasn't it? I hope you now take a moment to look up the Bible references, as they are very important. The point is simple: we can't do it on our own. Moving on from idolatrous patterns to godly ones takes the power and presence of the Holy Spirit. Moment by moment we are faced with choices that will take us either along the Spirit's path, or along the path of idol worship (Galatians 6:8).

### Led by the Spirit

Paul says that Christians are 'led by the Spirit' (Romans 8:14; Galatians 5:18). This doesn't mean primarily 'situational guidance' on matters such as whether I should wear red or blue socks,[7] or even guidance on bigger non-moral choices such as a surgeon deciding the next step in a delicate operation. Sometimes the Holy Spirit does guide us on such things, but that is not his main focus. With decisions like those, God expects us to use the minds he has given us and to exercise personal freedom.

So what does it mean to be 'led by the Spirit'? In both Romans and Galatians, leading by the Spirit is connected with personal Christlikeness, a change from self-centredness and idol-centredness to God-centredness and lives of love. The Holy Spirit has a vital role in that change process. He leads us through it, particularly in our attitudes and responses to life.

What is that like in practice? It means an inner awareness of the leadings and promptings of the Holy Spirit into a deeper sense of God's love, of our love for him and of confident, faith-driven love for others. We can expect him to be steering us away from idols and towards enjoying God and serving God instead.

### The Holy Spirit at breakfast

We should expect him to be bringing sentences or phrases from the Bible to our minds, not so much so that we can choose between eggs and bacon for breakfast, but so that we choose to wash up rather than leaving it to someone else, or choose not to get angry when we realize they have left their washing up from the night before. Those may seem unbearably trivial examples, but it is in the choices of life that the Holy Spirit leads and forms Christ in us. We don't make big choices all that often, but we make small but morally significant choices every day. And God has given us the Holy Spirit to lead us away from idolatrous choices (in their many forms) and into godly choices instead.

> Our sense of an alive, deepening relationship with God may arise
> . . . after an increase in our willingness or assent toward God.
> Perhaps we have released our hold on self a little or consciously
> invited God to be our all in all even when the risks of such
> surrender seemed high. Sometimes the Holy Spirit increases our
> awareness of God's love and quickens a kind of joy in us when
> we assent to the Spirit's invitations even in small ways.[8]

### Away from idols and into the fruit of the Spirit
We need to 'follow' his lead (Galatians 5:18). We need to listen to the inclinations and challenges he gives us. As we do, we can expect lovely fruit in our lives – love, joy, peace, patience, kindness, goodness, faithfulness, gentleness and self-control (Galatians 5:22–23) – the very opposite of what idolatry brings.

## The heart of idol busting
Here is the heart of idol busting: it is simply the gospel. Repentance, forgiveness, adoption and the Holy Spirit. Are you feeling discouraged about those idols? They seem so powerful. Are you worried about those idol habits? They seem to have enslaved you. How can you be free? Hear what God says:

It is for freedom that Christ has set us free. Stand firm, then, and
do not let yourselves be burdened again by a yoke of slavery.
(Galatians 5:1)

Stay free! Don't get burdened all over again, whether that
burden is your trying to keep the law to justify yourself, or the
old way of following idols.

In repentance and rest is your salvation,
   in quietness and trust is your strength,
   but you would have none of it.
(Isaiah 30:15)

## For discussion or personal reflection
Read Galatians 4:4–7.

1. What difference does being a child of God make to your
   life?
2. How could the truth of your adoption by God puncture
   the bubbles of your idols?
3. What is the connection between adoption and the Holy
   Spirit?
4. What is the role of the Holy Spirit in fighting idolatry?

## 14. A SUPREME AND SATISFYING LOVE

Remember our idol busting verse?

> This is what the Sovereign LORD, the Holy One of Israel, says:
> 'In repentance and rest is your salvation,
>    in quietness and trust is your strength,
>    but you would have none of it.'
> (Isaiah 30:15)

I always feel inadequate when authors tell me to learn verses. I have a hopeless memory for Bible verses. So at the danger of rank hypocrisy, I am going to suggest that you might like to try to learn this verse by repeating it over and over to yourself. I will try to do it myself, but if either of us doesn't make good progress with it, we won't condemn each other. Deal?

Our summary of idol busting is in this verse: repentance and rest. We are still on repentance, but rest keeps breaking through too! In our battle to break free, what we *think* matters immensely. Naturally our minds are wired all wrong. We think stupid things such as that we can get away with sin, or that sin will make us happy. We need those thoughts to be retuned so they are in tune with God and truth: 'be transformed by the renewing of your mind' (Romans 12:2). This is really a part of repentance. The word literally means a change of mind, a different way of thinking. The Bible doesn't use it only about a kind of change of opinion; as we have seen, it is broader than that. But repentance does involve a new way of thinking and that is crucial to change.

## Faulty mindset

We need it because our hearts are constantly creating illusions about created objects to make us put them in the spot reserved for God, the gift taking the rightful place of the Giver. They do this by telling us lies and capturing our imaginations so that the lies seem plausible. That is the chilling thing about the way the Israelites reject Isaiah in Isaiah 30: 'Tell us pleasant things, prophesy illusions!' It may be that Isaiah is mocking them: surely they couldn't actually have said that? Surely no-one could? But thoughts like that lay underneath their pushing him away. They didn't want to hear about what was right. Their hearts had been captured. Idols create patterns of false thinking that persuade us to act or feel in dysfunctional and idolatrous ways.

Having a third ice cream is not going to make me happy, but my sinful heart believes the lie: the look of the ice cream, the memory of the pleasure of the second one, and my sense of wanting something to make me happy conspire together to make me buy it and eat it . . . and then wish I hadn't!

### *Living the lie*

At root of all our life choices is a false belief system centred on an idol (or three) – the false belief that something other than God can give us the life, the joy, the hope and the truth that only God can give.[1] The Bible calls this a lie – 'they exchanged the truth about God for a lie' (Romans 1:25), or a set of 'empty words' (Ephesians 5:6). We believe the lie and dig the cisterns and drink the water.

All the possible causes of immorality – vulnerability, denial, emotional pain, etc. – really exist because in the midst of these risky places, we seek comfort and meaning apart from the Lord. We may be committed Christians who are trying to live as Christ would want, but we slip because we are functioning on a lie. That lie is, 'The answer to my problem [whatever it may be] lies in anything other than my relationship with Christ.'[2]

We need to correct our thinking. We need to stop believing the lie and start believing the truth. However, the way idols work is more than simply the input of false information at a rational level.

### It's all a dream

Your idols seem so persuasive. So credible. So plausible. But all they have is good presentational skills. What they promise is simply spin. It has no substance. They offer security, but they can't deliver. They offer pleasure, but it's only temporary and limited. They entice you with thoughts of exquisite enjoyment, or a deep calm peace, or a relief from the pain that is eating you up inside – but it's all a delusion.

> Tracy's home was immaculate. Her new kitchen was equipped with the latest gadgets. The lounge was large but cosy, always lovely and warm. There was a bedroom for every child and a spare and a study. Dinner party guests always exclaimed at the large, French polished table in the dining room. She and her husband had worked hard to get it all. Sometimes Tracey admitted to herself that it was funny how it left an empty feeling inside.

There's a great line in the romantic comedy film *Notting Hill*: it's spoken by a top film star who's seen through an illusion: 'You know the fame thing – it's not real.' Idols are the same – they're not real. What they offer, they can't deliver. We need to be convinced that we are accepted and secure in the love of God, which is more satisfying than anything any idol can ever give us.

### Can't get no satisfaction

The most crucial lie we believe is that idols will satisfy us. Actually, only God can. Moses was convinced of that. He asked God to:

> Satisfy us in the morning with your unfailing love,
> that we may sing for joy and be glad all our days.
> (Psalm 90:14)

This great request comes in a poem that reflects realistically and rather mournfully on life on earth in a fallen world: you read about it in Psalm 90:5–9. Moses seems to go out of his way to stress our frailty and the harshness of living in a world under God's judgment, a life that is 'nasty, brutish and short'.[3]

## Fighting for joy

However, Moses isn't content to leave it there. Moses is committed to a 'fight for joy'.[4] And Moses wants God to help him in his fight against moroseness and misery. Moses begs God to do something to lift him above his own natural melancholy so that he and his people might 'sing for joy and be glad all our days'.

His prayer is for God to satisfy them with his unfailing love. It is all the more remarkable because of the context of wrath, mortality and sin. In the real world, Moses dares to assert, we can live lives of gladness and joy when we are satisfied by the love of God. Do you believe that? Until you do, you'll keep those idols on the altar of your heart.

Why is God's love satisfying? The answer to that lies in Romans 8.

If God is for us, who can be against us? He who did not spare his own Son, but gave him up for us all – how will he not also, along with him, graciously give us all things? Who will bring any charge against those whom God has chosen? It is God who justifies. Who then can condemn? No-one. Christ Jesus who died – more than that, who was raised to life – is at the right hand of God and is also interceding for us. Who shall separate us from the love of Christ? Shall trouble or hardship or persecution or famine or nakedness or danger or sword? As it is written:

'For your sake we face death all day long;

we are considered as sheep to be slaughtered.'

No, in all these things we are more than conquerors through him who loved us. For I am convinced that neither death nor life, neither angels nor demons, neither the present nor the future, nor any powers, neither height nor depth, nor anything else in all creation, will be able to separate us from the love of God that is in Christ Jesus our Lord.

(Romans 8:31–39)

### Hold your breath!

What a breathtaking passage this part of Romans 8 is! This is the ultimate love letter: the God who gave us his Son, and gave him up to die for us, will never default on his promises to us. He will not condemn us; he will let nothing get in the way of his determined love. He promises unequivocally that nothing, absolutely nothing, can get between us and his love. Ever.

This is the Bible's 'Ode to Love', a soaring, magnificently orchestrated, faultlessly argued declaration that God will love us for ever and nothing can stop that. Truth and beauty combine here into the ultimate love song as the unshakable realities of the work of Christ send our souls soaring with the tunes of grace.

Paul asks five great questions.

- *Question 1*: Who can be against us if God is for us?

'For' means 'on our side'. There may be things against us, but which of them really matches God? God would have to be defeated for you to be defeated. Do you believe that? Put your name in the blank: God is for _____.

But how can I know that God is for me?

- *Question 2*: Seeing that God gave Jesus for us, won't he give us everything we could need?

The proof of God's love is in Jesus. He did not spare Jesus from the consequences of our sin. He gave him up to be punished on the cross for us, because he loved us and was determined to save us. What more proof can you need than that?

If he gave us his Son on the cross, is he really going to withhold anything we truly need? Do you really think so? Surely this shows that there is no outer limit to God's love. He will give us all those blessings, spiritual and material, that we require on the path towards our final salvation.[5]

But we say, 'I'm such a bad person!' Paul anticipates us in his next two questions.

- *Questions 3 and 4*: Who will bring any charge against us, since God has justifed us? Who is going to condemn us? Christ is for us.

We get so anxious and guilty about our sin. But Paul sees it differently. Imagine the prosecuting counsel, coming into court, loaded with files with long lists of sins – your sins! – and starting his opening speech. God dismisses it. 'I have justified him / her already!' he thunders. The verdict stands: 'Not guilty!' In a sense this says all that needs to be said, but Paul wants to ram it home.

Many Christians live under a cloud of condemnation. So he asks again, 'Who then can condemn?' The answer is, 'No-one.' No-one can. Because of Jesus, what he has done and where he is now. He died for our sins, was raised to new life and is now at God's right hand. What is he doing? What is his great work there? Making new supernovae? Planning the events of eternity? Maybe. But that is not what Paul says: his great work there is to pray for his people.[6] He is there praying for you. Making his work effective for ever.

### No condemnation

Pause for a moment to ask Paul's questions again: Who will bring any charge against you? Who is it who is condemning you?

### Safe in Christ: nothing can cut us off

But he can't leave it there. We live in a big bad world, full of cruelty and hardship, sudden illness and long-drawn-out pain. In it we face redundancy and bankruptcy and international terrorism and war and natural disasters. How can we cope with all this until heaven comes?

Like a kind mother who gives her frightened child a hug as well as a kiss, God gives us a further assurance of our security. Paul asks a final question.

- *Question 5*: Who shall separate us from the love of God?

It has a simple answer: 'Nothing!' But Paul is a good communicator and he wants us to think about all the things we fear so much. He gives a long list. It is worth thinking about these, because they are so often at the root of our idol worship.

- Trouble and hardship: they may be tough, but God's love is tougher still.

- Persecution: it will hurt, but God won't let us go.
- Famine and nakedness: so many of us fear going short, but even if we do, we'll still have God. If you were brought up in hard circumstances, the fear of them returning may underlie your idols.
- Danger and violence: people can do a lot to us, but they can't take God's love away from us.

He goes on: there is death – ours or some dear to us. But God goes on. Or life: sometimes life seems worse than death. But even the worst kind of living death can't separate us from his love. There is our present, where you are right now, where things are so bad you're not worried about the future: you wonder if you are going to make it to any future. But God's love is still with you. What about our future: how many idols do we worship because of our fear of the future? But the future is a land of God's love. In fact, there is nothing in the whole universe that can separate us from it.

### Your biggest fear
Which of these is your biggest fear? Face it honestly. It is much better to get it into the forefront of your mind. Otherwise it will lurk in the undergrowth and lure you into idolatry. Look it in the eyes in the presence of God and hear God's verdict: it cannot separate you from the love of God. It is strong, or you wouldn't be afraid of it – but his love is stronger.

### A love supreme
We need to hear this tune on Sundays and hum it on Mondays. We need our souls to be captured by this stunning reality. We need to believe it in our heads; feel it in our gut; follow it in our wills.
    John Coltrane was a jazz musician. He played saxophone

with some of the greats like Miles Davis and Dizzy Gillespie. He became very successful. But the high life took its toll. He developed a dependency on narcotic drugs. In the early 1950s he nearly died of a drugs overdose in San Francisco. When he recovered, he gave up both drugs and alcohol and came to put his faith in God. From his encounter with the living God came a piece called 'A Love Supreme'. It is a passionate, heartfelt, thirty-two-minute outpouring, thanking God for his blessing and offering him Coltrane's own soul. He had found the only true love supreme – in God.[7]

We will not overcome idols simply with behavioural change through resolution and willpower. Even if we get rid of one idol we will probably replace it with another. So instead of worshipping sex, for example, we start to idolize the god of our own moral performance. Changing one idol for another is like giving up burglary for a life of internet fraud.

Instead we need to be persuaded in heart, mind and imagination that God's love is the ultimate reality of our lives. That we are loved – loved more than we could ever have hoped for, loved with a love that is passionate and jealous and committed and powerful. That God knows our sense of need for security, control, approval, affection and comfort. That he meets those needs, as he sees best, in and through Christ.

### Dealing with those morning blues

> Satisfy us in the morning with your unfailing love,
>     that we may sing for joy and be glad all our days.
> (Psalm 90:14)

Notice the timing of this prayer: 'satisfy us in the morning'. I think Moses may have been thinking like this: those morning blues – how hard is it to wake up and be glad when life is so fragile? I need to fight for joy, but I need God's help and I need it in this specific way: I need to be satisfied in his love, the love that never fails, that never runs dry, that never wavers and never needs rebooting. Of course, when I start to think of it, it is satisfying, but I need his help to see it freshly and for it to capture my heart all over again.

Repentance from fear and reaching to idols to secure approval or comfort or hope. Resting in God's invincible, committed love. That's how to bust those idols!

Ian's job in the high-tech start-up company wasn't great. He'd had such high hopes, but the plans for him that his manager had beamed about at the interview never materialized. He often felt bored and useless. Changing wasn't an option in the present economic climate. He began to simmer with resentment: the job had let him down badly and it felt as though his whole life had been ruined. Outwardly he smiled in meetings; inwardly he fumed. Then the vicar read Psalm 90 as part of his sermon. Verse 14 hit Ian with a hurricane force: God's love was what should satisfy him. It helped him realize that he'd placed too much expectation on the job and not enough on God.

## For discussion or personal reflection
Read Romans 8:31–39.

1. Which of your deep fears does Paul list?
2. How are these overcome in Christ?
3. Think of some deep idols: security, control, comfort, approval. How does this passage give you these things in Christ?
4. What stops you from being satisfied by God's love?

## 15. REST INSTEAD OF RESTLESSNESS

How is the idol busting going? Don't get too impatient. Remember it takes time. It won't happen in a week, but over a month you may see real progress. Remember our lead idol busting verse?

> This is what the Sovereign LORD, the Holy One of Israel, says:
> 'In repentance and rest is your salvation,
>     in quietness and trust is your strength.'
> (Isaiah 30:15)

How are you doing with learning it? I'm struggling too.

### Rest

We have looked at the importance of repentance and all it brings to us. Now let's think about rest. Release from idol worship comes in new habits of our hearts. We need to replace our feverish drives to serve our idols with rest in Christ. Jesus himself invites us to that specifically:

> At that time Jesus said . . . 'Come to me, all you who are weary and burdened, and I will give you rest. Take my yoke upon you and learn from me, for I am gentle and humble in heart, and you will find rest for your souls. For my yoke is easy and my burden is light.'
> (Matthew 11:25, 28–30)

### Idol burdens

Idolatry typically gives us a burden that leaves us weary. We are yoked – that is, we can't get away from our idols. Jesus knows: he's seen it all around him. He is perhaps thinking particularly of the burden of the idol of religious activity, the effort of law-keeping and self-justification. But more widely, *all* idols have yokes and burdens. They are hard taskmasters with worn-out slaves.

> Dave had to take time off work: he'd been overdoing it and the long hours had caught up with him. Lots of his friends from church sent him cards and emails. Several of them included Matthew 11:28: 'Come unto me and rest.' He got a bit fed up with it. 'OK, OK,' he said to himself, 'I'm trying my hardest.' Then one day, while he was out for a walk as the GP had advised, he got it properly: it wasn't just resting that mattered, but resting in Christ.

Take a moment to think of the way idols burden you. Be honest about the yoke you have put yourself under to serve them.

### A better way

Jesus promises a better way: serving him while resting in him. In the next chapters we see four of the Bible's idol busters. They are four habits of life that enable us to make rest in Christ a reality.

- Drawing near to God.
- Gazing on the face of Jesus.
- Submitting to the will and word of God.
- Looking forward to the glory of God.

### Time with God
The first two of these involve, though are not limited to, our private devotional times. I expect your alarm bells to start going off now! You know from experience that at some point every Christian author is going to tell you that you need to have better times of prayer. You also know that it is going to make you feel guilty.

### That guilty look
I know this from pastoral experience. When I ask people how their walk with the Lord is, they almost invariably look shifty and talk about how hard it is to find time to pray every day. I never even mentioned 'quiet times', and they are already explaining why they don't have them! I have to work hard to show that I am not like some spiritual foreman, checking when they have clocked in and out with God.

### A new approach
I don't want to make you feel guilty. I don't want to give you a new burden. I want to suggest to you that you should think of devotional times as times of drawing near to God and gazing on the face of Christ. Be honest for a moment. Is that how you think of them?

### Why Sam couldn't get up to pray
In a powerful illustration, one writer analyses a common approach to times of personal prayer, in the life of the well-known eighteenth-century character Samuel Johnson, creator of the first English dictionary and a professing Christian.[1] If you read Johnson's journals, apparently you can see a repeated pattern over the years of him resolving to get up earlier to pray and failing to do so. There may, of course, be many reasons for this, but it may well be that the heart of it was that

he was coming to God not as a son but as a servant. He was weighed down with a sense of failure, but he did not have the assurance that his sins were forgiven through Christ's death. He even thought the cross wasn't powerful enough for sins as bad as his. He was ashamed to come to God. He did not relate to God as a heavenly Father.

### Servant or child?

What about you? Do you relate to God as your Father? He certainly is your Father if you have trusted Christ. But do you relate to him that way as you think about prayer? Or is your quiet time more of a spiritual 'exercise', reading a set number of verses or (for the really keen) chapters of the Bible, praying through a list of names, asking for help for the hard-looking bits of the day ahead, perhaps remembering the guy in your house group who has flu?

### Why prayer times drag

I am totally convinced that many, many Christians find devotions hard because that is what they are doing in them when they have them. They are relating to God as failing, unforgiven servants. Who wouldn't find that hard? If that is you, no wonder you find these times difficult. And you will also find it hard to bust your idols. I want to suggest that you start all over again, like this: think of your devotions as time to draw near to God and gaze on the face of Jesus Christ.

## Drawing near to the presence of God

Have you ever wondered what on earth the book of Hebrews is about? This next sentence is a pretty good summary!

> Therefore, brothers and sisters, since we have confidence to enter the Most Holy Place by the blood of Jesus, by a new and living

way opened for us through the curtain, that is, his body, and since we have a great priest over the house of God, let us draw near to God with a sincere heart in full assurance of faith, having our hearts sprinkled to cleanse us from a guilty conscience and having our bodies washed with pure water.

(Hebrews 10:19–22)

This very long sentence has one key thought: 'Let us draw near to God.' The writer contrasts the Old Testament system, where only the high priest could enter the special holy place at the centre of the temple, with the New Covenant brought in by Jesus. Now, anyone who is a Christian has access into the very presence of God anywhere, anytime. It's rather like wireless broadband internet access. All we have to do is open our spiritual browser by praying, and there we are, in his presence.

### The sympathetic Master

Earlier in the book, the author uses the same idea.

We do not have a high priest who is unable to feel sympathy for our weaknesses, but we have one who has been tempted in every way, just as we are – yet he did not sin. Let us then approach God's throne of grace with confidence, so that we may receive mercy and find grace to help us in our time of need.

(Hebrews 4:15–16)

Hard times make most of us wobble spiritually. So do our failures. We may want to resort to an idol that will give us some kind of comfort or distraction. We may think that God doesn't care about the hardship and condemns us for the failure. Actually it's the opposite. He does sympathize: he's been through hard times too. And he has dealt with the failure. All in Jesus. So our sadness and our sins should drive us sprinting into the arms of God. Our times of need are when we should draw near all the more: only in his presence will we find the mercy and grace we need.

### Failures welcomed!

Sins also make us wobble. We feel that the presence of God is the last place we deserve to be. So it is. But Jesus' death has reversed that. If we feel we are unworthy, we can rest in the assurance of guilty consciences that have been cleansed. The battered, sad, tear-stained, disobedient child finds a ready welcome and a big hug in its mother's arms. So do we from God.

This is how one person draws near:

I stop.
I remember the holy place with the curtain in the Old Testament.
I remember the work of Christ.
I remember that the heavenly curtain is open.
I remember that Christ is beckoning me into the heavenly throne
    room of God.
I remember that God is expecting me, beckoning me, welcoming me.

I allow my mind to focus on him.

I find that I am there. And I simply rest there.

I remember his promises to me.
I recall Christ's finished work for me.
His greatness overwhelms me.
I worship him.

I let my mind return to my troubles.
I bring him whatever is troubling me.
I remember that he went through troubles too.
I tell myself that he sympathizes with me.
I remember all my weaknesses.

Usually this makes things worse but in God's presence
    I remember that Jesus had weaknesses too.
It helps.
A lot.

I find my fears stilled.
I find my heart being retuned.
Somehow it's now easier to be patient.
It is easier to trust.
It is easier to forgive.
It is easier to live for God because I am living close to God.

### Anywhere, any time

What a huge privilege: to be able to draw near to God any-where, any time. We don't have to be in a church building. Special people like priests or pastors aren't needed to take us there. We can just close our eyes (you don't even have to close your eyes, but it can help to focus your thoughts) and draw near by taking mental steps of faith towards God. And he is there. Sometimes we feel it more than others, but he is always there. Now that is worth getting up for!

### God showed me Hebrews

I never really saw this until I had to preach on Hebrews for some students. I say 'had to', because the person or committee organizing the event announced that the talks would be on Hebrews and then told *me*. So I was stuck with it. A book I had never studied, or understood. What else could I do? Emigrate? Turn up with some talks on Ephesians? Pretend to be ill?

### Hebrews unfolded

I decided I'd have a go at Hebrews and I spent most of four weeks of summer sabbatical time studying it. I learned a lot,

but by far the most important thing I found was that Christ
had died to make it possible for me to draw near to God and
that if I was going to keep going in the Christian life I had to
*keep* drawing near to God. It transformed my devotional life.

### That daily drawing near
I believe it is a vital weapon in our battle with idolatry. Drawing
near to God stills our hearts and brings us sympathy, help and
mercy (Hebrews 4:14–16). Why don't we do it daily? Why not
give it a try? Remember that it is by faith, ask the Holy Spirit
to help you. And give it at least a week, preferably two. See
what God can do.

### In his presence
What do we do when we draw near? We could answer that
by recalling the first set of idol busters: repentance, assurance
of forgiveness and being God's child; following the Holy
Spirit's lead and depending on him. But I want to focus specifically on Jesus and suggest that when we draw near, we should
look at him.

## For discussion or personal reflection
Read Hebrews 4:14–16.

1. Think about a situation where an idolatrous thought or
   deed seems very attractive. How could these verses help
   you to put God back on his throne?
2. What would your life look like if you came to God's
   throne with confidence more often?
3. Was Jesus tempted by idols? Can you think of any
   specific examples? How does Jesus' own experience help
   you? Why is it important that he was 'without sin'?

## Then I saw his face

I heard a comedy show on the radio where panellists had to summarize a whole book in a couple of lines from a pop song. I can't remember any of them except one. This guy had been challenged to do 'The Bible'. Of course everyone tittered. His reply was brilliant: 'Then I saw his face / Now I'm a believer.' The song was by The Monkees, not the most long-lasting or profound of cultural products, though this is one of their better songs.[1] But it was a great answer – not complete, of course, and in the original it was 'Then I saw *her* face', but with a surprising level of understanding. Why? Because the heart of the Bible is that Jesus became a man; as we gaze by faith on his crucified but risen face, we believe and are changed. It reminded me of this great verse in Paul:

> And we all, who . . . contemplate the Lord's glory, are being transformed into his image with ever-increasing glory, which comes from the Lord, who is the Spirit.
> (2 Corinthians 3:18)

The key words here are 'contemplate' and 'transformed'. Those who *contemplate* the glory of Christ are *transformed* by it. No contemplation, no transformation.

This is especially important in the battle against idolatry. Otherwise we may simply try to use human willpower – but it is very difficult to put something out of your mind unless you have something else to put in its place.

## Interlude for chocolate-free thought

Try it for a moment. I want you to avoid thinking about chocolate. You can have anything in your mind except chocolate. Don't think about Mars Bars, or Milk Tray, or Bendicks Bittermints.[2]

How's it going? Not very well? It's hard, isn't it!

Now think about a beach you've enjoyed being on. The waves are crashing with white surf. Sunshine is sparkling off the surface of the water. The cries of seagulls fill the air. You can feel the sun on your back and the sand between your toes. Over to your left a family is playing cricket; on your right some children are splashing around in rock pools. The holiday is just beginning.

So how did that go? Whether or not you like beaches, I bet you didn't think much about chocolate.

## Gazing at Jesus, not idols

The idols of our hearts have taken God's place, attracting us with false promises of substitute glory. We need to feel the superior glory of Jesus Christ. We need to see that glory by faith. More than seeing is needed: we need to enjoy the beauty that is there, recognizing the true worth of Christ.

### Gazing, not glazing over

Notice the effect that gazing at Jesus has: Paul says it 'transforms us'. Remember that we become like what we worship. If we revere idols, we start to resemble them and become hollowed out and unreal. But if we gaze at Jesus, we become like him. We actually become 'his image'. This is God's great plan for us: 'those God foreknew he also pre-destined to be conformed to the image of his Son' (Romans 8:29).[3] That is the great antidote to idols: putting Christ back in his place and enjoying his glory and letting it transform us.

In the film *Educating Rita*, the heroine, Rita, has to find a new place to live. She answers an advert, goes round to the house, and the door is opened to a blast of music. 'Don't you just love Mahler?' says her prospective housemate, Trish. Rita is bowled over by Trish's poise and sophistication. Later, though, Trish is found with a bottle of pills next to her bed and the record deck turning soundlessly. She had tried to use constant stimulation to drown out her inner life, but in the end she couldn't.

I wonder how much we all use our inputs to drown our fears – and also to shut out the very thing that might overcome them: the Holy Spirit showing us Jesus.

### Getting practical

How can you do that practically? First of all, it does not mean using pictures of Jesus, either physical ones or ones in our memories or minds. We have to be very careful about breaking the Second Commandment not to make images of God to worship. I don't think this necessarily means that all artistic representations of Jesus are wrong: they have their uses. But surely it means that we should not use them in this kind of contemplation.

### God's Facebook

Instead we need to think of the Bible as a 'Facebook'. God has revealed himself through words, not pictures, but the words show us Jesus' face so that by faith we can have a relationship with him.

A Scottish minister in the nineteenth century called Murray McCheyne had a friend who was also a minister. His friend tended to get anxious and fret about things. Murray McCheyne wrote to him to try to help him with this. He wrote a letter to him including this sentence: 'For every look you take at yourself, take ten at Christ. He is altogether lovely . . . Live much in the smiles of God. Bask in his [sun]beams. Feel his all-seeing eye settled on you in love, and repose in his mighty arms.'[4]

### Choosing to think Jesus

As well as reading the Bible and thinking about its words, we need actively to bring Christ to mind. We need to take time just to bring the glory of Christ into our minds and to fix our thoughts on him. It is especially helpful if we tend to think too much about ourselves, or our idols, or just stuff.

Simply bringing Christ to mind more is a radical move for most of us. Fix your thoughts on his glory with the Father in heaven, his descent to earth as a man, his life for you and his death for you, his resurrection, his place next to God on the throne of the universe, where he is praying for you. Think about his love, not just in general, but for you in particular – he is the Son of God who loved you and gave himself for you (Galatians 2:20). Feast your thoughts on what he has in store for you.

### Idol comparison

Then compare him with your idols. Be active here. You will have to recall the idolatrous patterns you have diagnosed and bring them to mind. Think how much more satisfying he is than acquiring new gadgets or clothes. Put his love next to the things you use to comfort you. Then apply his promises to those deep idols: security, power, approval, comfort, control. Thank him that you have total security in him. Thank him that you don't need to be powerful because he is powerful and works in your weakness. Thank him that he has accepted you, for ever, so there is no condemnation in your life. Thank him that he gives you so much that brings you comfort; that even if it was all taken away, you would still have him; that one day it will be all comfort, in his presence for ever. Praise him that his total control over your life means that you don't have to fear losing control or strive to gain control, but can live in a more relaxed way, stepping out of your comfort zone in faith as he calls you.

### Mental space

I wrote most of this chapter staying in a cottage in North Wales lent me by kind friends for a week all on my own. Before I came, I decided to try keeping things a bit more simple. So no radio. No TV. No newspaper. No internet. I am a complete news junkie: this was a radical simplification of my inputs! I also thought I'd try keeping my meals as simple as possible: no meat, no frills.

It was a good week. I learned a lot about myself. What I gained more than anything else was mental space to fill with Jesus. To be honest, I was rather horrified to discover how much of my mental activity is normally taken up with a kind of feverish focus on news, sport and Google searches for things of interest.

### Don't go monastic

Being an introvert, I am the sort of person who can enjoy being alone for a week. I have friends who are extroverts who would have ended up insane. So I am not saying that a week of solitary confinement is the way forward – and actually I couldn't and wouldn't want to live like that either, but there is perhaps something to learn from it.

### Input overload
One of the features of our age is the way we fill our minds with noise and sensation and stimulation all day. Newspapers, TV, radio, hi-fi – those are just the old-fashioned inputs. The internet has added a new dimension or two to the possibilities: news, information, YouTube, Google, Facebook, Spotify – and probably something new and dazzling between the writing and printing of this book! All of this is potentially great. But cumulatively it has an effect. It crowds out the Holy Spirit.

## Idol busters through idleness?
Some people think of meditation and stillness before God as rather idle pursuits. They are like Martha, who wanted Mary to help her in the kitchen rather than sitting looking at Jesus and listening to him. But Jesus said that Mary had chosen the 'better' thing (Luke 10:38–42). He added that it would not be taken away from her – presumably by Martha or himself. However, we can take it away from ourselves. Many of us do. And we wonder why we find idols attractive! Use the idol buster! Learn to draw near to God and gaze by faith on the glory of Christ. Learn the importance of 'being' rather than 'doing'.[5]

## For discussion or personal reflection
Read Matthew 11:25–30.

1. What has made you weary and burdened?
2. Think deeply: what is the idol-driven restlessness that underlies your weariness and your burdens?
3. What does Christ offer instead?

4. Choose one of these and discuss or think about how you can develop this weapon in your fight against the deep idols of your heart.
5. Meditating on the glory of Christ and drawing near to the presence of God can transform our quiet times. What would that look like for you?
6. What would it mean for you to 'be' rather than to 'do'?

## 17. SUBMISSION TO GOD'S WILL AND WORD

In our idol busting, we have taken one verse as our guide: Isaiah 30:15. Perhaps it's even starting to stick in your mind a bit?

> In repentance and rest is your salvation,
> > in quietness and trust is your strength . . .

I wonder if you have forgotten the end of it. It is easy to leave it out:

> . . . but you would have none of it.

### Turning God down

The tragedy of the generation Isaiah was addressing is that they had this great offer, but they wouldn't take it. They rejected it. They didn't want to submit to God, even when he was offering them salvation. Salvation means submission. When Jesus offered rest to any weary person who wanted it, he wasn't offering them control of their lives. We weren't made to run our own lives. That's why we worship idols. And that is why salvation from idols means a new, better, easy yoke and a completely different kind of burden – from Jesus himself. In the first part of this chapter we are going to look at part of that yoke.

## Submitting to the discipline and will of God

### Church in turmoil

Holy Trinity Church was under pressure. Some of the members
had been thrown in prison. Since then things had eased, but
there were still plenty of church members whose families
mocked them for their faith. The future didn't look too bright
either. Rumblings from governmental circles suggested a fresh
crackdown on religious groups who wouldn't buy into the
prevailing religious pluralism. One Sunday they opened a letter
from a former pastor. Part of it read:

> Have you completely forgotten this word of encouragement that
> addresses you as children? It says,
>> 'My son, do not make light of the Lord's discipline,
>>> and do not lose heart when he rebukes you,
>> because the Lord disciplines those he loves,
>>> and he chastens everyone he accepts as his child.'
> Endure hardship as discipline; God is treating you as his children.
> For what children are not disciplined by their father? If you are not
> disciplined – and everyone undergoes discipline – then you are not
> legitimate children at all. Moreover, we have all had parents who
> disciplined us and we respected them for it. How much more should
> we submit to the Father of spirits and live! Our parents disciplined us
> for a little while as they thought best; but God disciplines us for our
> good, that we may share in his holiness. No discipline seems pleasant
> at the time, but painful. Later on, however, it produces a harvest of
> righteousness and peace for those who have been trained by it.
> (Hebrews 12:5–11)

### Not what we want to hear

OK, they weren't called Holy Trinity, but everything else about
them is pretty much true as we read in the letter to the Hebrews.

Perhaps the fact that they knew this man helped them to stomach his words. We don't know him, but we have to read and learn from his words too. It takes some effort, because what he says is tough stuff: 'Put up with your suffering, because God is using it to train you: he does it because he is your loving Father and he wants you to be like him.'

### Submission

The response he is after is in verse 9: we should 'submit to the Father of [our] spirits and live!' 'Submission' isn't a word we instinctively warm to: it sounds like 'submersion' and most of us would just as rather be submersed in freezing water than submit to anyone. We cherish our independence and freedom. But the Bible is very big on submission – especially our submitting to God.

> Scripture says:
>    'God opposes the proud
>       but shows favour to the humble and oppressed.'
> Submit yourselves, then, to God.
> (James 4:6–7)

This reference in Hebrews is very telling. Submit to him. What does it mean? In context it is clear that we submit to God by 'enduring hardship as discipline' (v. 7). That is, by a conscious, deliberate choice, we accept what happens in our lives as part of God's training programme to make us like him, to make us resemble him ('that we may share in his holiness', v. 10).

### Submission is tough!

I know how hard that can be. A few years ago I was really struggling with thwarted ambition. There was a job I wanted and God wasn't giving it to me. He seemed to be putting up every roadblock you could imagine in my way. It made me sad, frustrated, angry and confused. Then out of nowhere I picked up a set of sermons preached in the seventeenth century called 'Of Walking Humbly with God'.[1] The preacher takes 'walking humbly with God'[2] to be, fundamentally, submitting to God's will and accepting it, even when it isn't what we would have chosen, when it frankly makes us howl, and when we can't see where it is going.

### A micro death[3]

That felt like ego death to me. It was. Because it was also death to an idol in which I was investing my hopes. People love idols because they think that investing in them will produce a desired outcome. But submitting to God means trusting *him* to make us happy, not our idols. It was also a huge test of faith, because I had to believe that God was using something deeply undesirable to bring about something good for me. That sounds horrid, doesn't it? What kind of father would do that?

Down the ages, child after child of God has been through hard times and in the end has praised him for what they brought. One Scottish leader imagined himself in a workshop and his sufferings as God's tools: 'Oh, what I owe to the file, to the hammer, to the furnace of my Lord Jesus!'[4]

### Suffering neutralizes idols

God can use hardship to liberate us from different kinds of idolatry. Michelle Graham had a friend who was, let us say, over-concerned about her appearance. She was a preener and fusser. Then she had an accident which left her with a broken arm. As a result, preening became rather hard. She struggled with looking frumpy, but eventually found a wonderful liberation from the need to look great.[5]

Some of us pride ourselves on our independence. We won't ask for help – or accept it. Our self-sufficiency becomes an idol. In the end God will have to use something to challenge that. Something happens which means that we simply have to ask for help! It is the sort of thing that Paul calls a 'thorn in the flesh' in 2 Corinthians 12. And the result is that we lose an idol and gain new depth in friendship, 'establishing a special and solid bond with a few very significant people . . . in a rich, meaningful relationship that was unthinkable without the thorn'.[6]

Mike Mason tells the story of a friend, also called Mike, who was unemployed for a long time. It raised all sorts of issues for him. He wondered what he could possibly do to justify his existence with all the time on his hands. Challenged by his pastor in a sermon, Mike asked God to speak to him. What he felt God saying was this: 'This is a time to focus on your wife and children. Learn to love them more deeply. Work is of very little importance to Me. What's important to Me is people.'[7]

A friend of mine found out that his wife had cancer. It was agonizing. In the middle of the tests and the upheaval, as he cried out to God, God asked my friend to trust him, simply to trust him whatever happened. He responded with faith. His wife did make a recovery and he found he had learned something:

I had nearly lost her and still might not have her for long, we had been through a time of great suffering, and yet I felt (I can only put it this way) as if I *weighed* more for the experience I had had and the situation I was in. It was as if I was a more complete person for having been in such deep waters, as if I was more valuable to others and even to God in the life that stretched before me, a wiser and perhaps weightier man.[8]

Frank couldn't believe it. God had let him down *again*. It felt as though he had been led up the garden path and into a bog. There was this girl, Imogen. She was on another course, but he had met her at Christian Union. He'd liked her from the start: pretty, godly, quiet and sensitive, just the right foil for his liveliness. He knew better than to jump right in: he would wait and pray. For two terms he did just that. He waited – boy, was it hard. He prayed – asking for God's guidance. Eventually he felt that God was leading him. So he told Imogen he liked her and asked her out. Her response was devastating: 'Oh, Frank, I've never thought of you that way.' And she didn't start thinking of him that way either. He was devastated. A friend listened to him and then said, 'You know, you do have a choice. You can fight God, or you can submit to his will.' Frank felt like hitting him, but he knew which would be best. Later he found he had learned something through the experience and he used to tell people, 'I never realized God loved me enough to put me through that kind of pain.'

### Restful obedience

Submitting is more than passivity, however: there is an active submission to the will of God in our fight against idols. Submitting to God also means allowing his word rather than our idolatrous desires to shape our lives. Remember how Jesus called us to find rest in him an 'easy yoke' and a 'light burden' (Matthew 11:28–30)? The yoke and burden are the commandments of Jesus, summarized as loving God with all our heart and loving other people as we love ourselves. On first sight that looks incredibly hard! Much harder than making sure you had washed your hands the right number of times or tithed your herbs, as the Pharisees taught.

### New covenant life

So what does Jesus mean? I think what he must mean is that there is a simplicity and wholeness about the new covenant love command. We don't have to worry about endless regulations: we have a big picture that applies to everything. But there is more than that. These are not simply commandments in a rule book or on tablets of stone. They are written on our hearts (Jeremiah 31:33), 'not with ink but with the Spirit of the living God' (2 Corinthians 3:3), and 'where the Spirit of the Lord is, there is freedom' (2 Corinthians 3:17) in the 'new covenant – not of the letter but of the Spirit; for the letter kills, but the Spirit gives life' (2 Corinthians 3:6).

The Holy Spirit brings a whole new dynamic into play. He leads, he enables, he transforms. What about us? We have to be open to his work. We have to keep in step with him. As we do that, we find we can love God and our neighbour.

This is an antidote to our idols, because so often they are highly self-centred. Jesus' love command orientates us outward. Instead of thinking about our own needs, we focus on others and the idol is displaced.

So ask the Holy Spirit to empower you to submit to God's discipline and to submit to his word too.

## For discussion or personal reflection

Read James 1:2–7.

1. Why should Christians be joyful at trying times?
2. Why is it so hard?
3. Why is it worth it?
4. How has God used hardship to dislodge idols in your life?

## 18. LOOKING FORWARD TO THE GLORY OF GOD

My father died in December 2008 and I found myself an heir. I've been walking around in a coat of his that I rather liked. He had an old fountain pen that I had idly hoped to get my hands on one day. Unfortunately, it doesn't hold ink any more. No joy there. However, much more significant is the inheritance I have in Jesus Christ, and so do you, an inheritance of undiluted and intense joy.

> Now if we are children, then we are heirs – heirs of God and co-heirs with Christ, if indeed we share in his sufferings in order that we may also share in his glory. I consider that our present sufferings are not worth comparing with the glory that will be revealed in us.
> (Romans 8:17–18)

### Why it matters
This is very important in our idol busting, because the attraction of idols is so often relief from our sadness. They zoom in on our unhappiness and fears, but lure us into further doubt or fear. To counter them we need a living experience of joy in Christ. But that is never total.

### Mixed emotions
In this life we never experience perfect, undiluted, simple, pure joy without any negative emotion. At least not for very long.

In this life there is always a mixture.[1] Although we are able to experience 'an inexpressible and glorious joy' (1 Peter 1:8), Paul reminds us that there are also groans and there is sadness. Straight after he calls the Romans to 'rejoice with those who rejoice', Paul says they must also 'mourn with those who mourn' (Romans 12:15). Until Jesus comes again, our inner life will never be pure joy and we should beware of teachers and song-writers who claim that it is! Paul himself said, 'We ourselves, who have the firstfruits of the Spirit, groan inwardly' (Romans 8:23).

### Groaning

Even though we have the Holy Spirit, we still groan! Christians groan – and not just at bad jokes either, or just at our own sin. We groan at that sciatic pain down our leg that the physio's best efforts can't remove. We groan at our friend's suffering with a disabled child. We groan at pictures of exploitation and deprivation in other countries which we see on the TV. Groaning is normal and groaning is real.

### Groaning: an opportunity for idols

The danger is that we will allow our sadness to tempt us – to anaesthetize that pain with a 'quick' visit to an internet porn site or to a sly binge-eating session. Groaning may leave us doubting God, cynical, embittered and hardened. But there is a better way.

### Using groans to fight idolatry

The groans can help us fight idols rather than leading us to succumb to them. We need to groan our groans and moan our moans in a new way – not as a miserable outpouring of our frustration with life, but as a longing for something better *that is on its way*:

> We ourselves, who have the firstfruits of the Spirit, groan inwardly
> as we wait eagerly for our adoption, the redemption of our bodies.
> (Romans 8:23)

We need to realize that our groans are the groans of the marathon runner who is closing in on the final lap. He's entered the stadium, the crowd are roaring him on, the nearest rival is two miles back and he has enough energy in his legs to make it to the finishing line and win gold. Yes, he groans – who wouldn't? – but he knows the groans will become glory within a few short strides.

### Wise words from Winslow

We have a greater glory: our adoption as sons and daughters and the redemption of our bodies. All that is summed up in this way:

> Our present sufferings are not worth comparing with the glory
> that will be revealed in us.
> (Romans 8:18)

An old writer called Octavius Winslow wrote a book on Romans 8 in which he included a powerful, inspiring section on the glory to come. He sums this verse up in ten words:

> One second of glory will extinguish a lifetime of suffering.[2]

I repeat that sentence a lot in our church when I preach on suffering. I suspect that most of the regulars know it by heart by now. I hope they do. Glory – future glory, perfect glory, our glory. It will be worth it! And it will wipe out all the groans – so that we don't deflect our attention from where it should be. Look at verse 17:

We share in his sufferings in order that we may also share in his glory.

We have a share, a tiny share, in the future glory of Jesus Christ. But overwhelmingly the main glory is his and his alone. We will experience a little of it in the renewed bodies we'll enjoy. We reflect all we can of it. And we simply enjoy it.

Mary found it very difficult that she was the only one of three sisters who wasn't married. Jean met Harry at university: they had started a family early and now had three children of their own. True, Mary's other sister, Edith, had to wait a little longer, but eventually she'd found Mark (Mary suspected it was through an internet dating site) and they got married last summer. It wasn't as though Mary had suffered any shortage of guys asking her out. Plenty of work colleagues and fellow salsa dancers had tried. But she'd turned them all down. None of them was a Christian and she knew she could only marry a Christian. Often she felt very lonely; and Christmas at her parents was rather mixed. One day the music group at church introduced a new song. It asked, 'How long?' Mary was struck by one of the lines: 'How long? 'til the widow finds a husband who will never leave her side.'*

She found it rather comforting. Not that it was promising a husband, nor that she was a widow (as if!). But the thought that when Jesus came back (whenever that was) she wouldn't feel lonely any more helped her to start Monday much more brightly than the week before. Next time she started to feel sorry for herself, she hummed the tune.

* 'We Have Sung Our Songs Of Victory' by Stuart Townend, copyright © 1997 Thankyou Music.

### The end is near

That is what lies ahead. So we can endure the sufferings, the frustrations, the groans, the pains. There is something worth enduring them for – and we do not need to turn to idols to distract us or help us through.

### Future glory and your idols

Apply this to your idols for a moment. Idols often captivate us because we are fearful about the future. If only we invest a bit more or avoid taking a risk for God, we may make it secure. God simply says that he will provide for our needs, without any guarantee that we won't face illness or shortage, but with a promise that one day, all that suffering will end. Which of your idols can offer that? Isn't permanent, perfect joy what your idols are whispering to you about? But where else will you find it? Doesn't that mean that for a few years at least, you can put up with some hardship without resorting to idolatrous distractions or even diversions from God's will for your life?

This is the last of our idol busting chapters. There could have been several more. I am rather painfully aware how much more I could and perhaps should have said, of the gaps and omissions, for you really need all the promises and commandments of God!

### Resting and trusting

But let's return to our lead verse.

> This is what the Sovereign LORD, the Holy One of Israel, says:
> 'In repentance and rest is your salvation,
>> in quietness and trust is your strength,
>> but you would have none of it.
> (Isaiah 30:15)

He's offering you rest in submission to his will, even if the way is hard. He's saying there is strength in him if you will quietly trust in his coming glory. Put your need for comfort in this life alongside those promises.

## For discussion or personal reflection
Read Revelation 22:1–6.

1. What are you most looking forward to in the new creation when Christ returns?
2. How can this shape your attitude to life now, especially in relation to idols?

## 19. YOU'RE SO VAIN, YOU PROBABLY THINK THIS BOOK IS ABOUT YOU

I couldn't resist adapting perhaps the cleverest title of any pop song ever: 'You're So Vain You Probably Think This Song Is About You'. Carly Simon wrote and sang it, but she has never admitted who the song is actually about. That's the point – not to give the cheating, lying man the satisfaction of knowing it was him and at the same time shaming every man who ever let her down. Clever . . .[1]

But before we get onto that, I want to try to pull things together. In a way, of course, this book *is* about you and for you. Let me try to summarize what I hope it has done for you.

### Idols according to Bruce

One of the qualities of Bruce Springsteen's music is his ability to tell (with deep compassion) the stories of ordinary people, with their thwarted ambitions and dashed hopes. Theologically, we can see that these characters are idolaters whose idols have left them hollow. In song after song, he laments their shattered dreams. 'The Promised Land'[2] describes idols better than any theologian as 'dreams that tear you apart' and 'break your heart'; they are 'the lies that leave you nothing but lost and broken-hearted'. That is what our idols are: false dreams and lies which tear us and break us.

### Redemption

Bruce's characters long for redemption from their disappointment. In 'The Promised Land', he imagines a dark cloud, a
tornado, rising from the surface of the desert, to blow the
deceptive dreams and lies away. There is a confident proclam-
ation that he believes in a 'Promised Land'. But when you
listen carefully and probe beneath the images, in the end it's
just cars and girls – new idols, new disappointments in store.
The 'runaway American dream' of 'Born To Run' can't last
for ever. Eventually the gas runs out or the travellers get weary.
For we are not, not even Bruce, born to run, we are born to
worship – born to worship the living God and him alone.

However, there *is* good news. There *is* a wind to blow the
dreams and the lies away: the wind of the Holy Spirit, who
blows where he will and turns our lives upside down. When
he applies the realities of the gospel of Jesus Christ to our
hearts we will find progressive release from the disappointments and hollowness that our idols have given us. As he
focuses our lives on God, we will really live.

### Our mistakes are no longer our destiny

Jean-Paul Sartre asserted that a person 'struggles with all his
strength against the crushing view that his mistakes constitute
his destiny'.[3] Many of us think that our mistakes or our parents'
mistakes determine our lives. They do not have to any more.
In the mirror of the Bible we see that our mistakes are the
result of the strange worship of false gods. We all have idols
which dethrone God, disappoint and destroy us, and Jesus
Christ came to change that.

### It was for freedom . . .

Jesus came to release us from that self-imposed destiny of
disappointment and destruction. God – Father, Son and Spirit

– committed himself in eternity to a powerful intervention to recapture our hearts. In the message of the gospel we find deliverance. You can break free! Things can be different. The hollowness and pain your idols have brought can be changed. Renewal and improvement are real possibilities if you cooperate with the Holy Spirit in bringing them and are open to his leading.

### Heart recapture

Do you realize that God wants to recapture your heart?[4] He is determined to win it back from those precious, familiar, cosy, dearly loved, comforting but deceptive and ultimately disappointing idols. You have seen something better than idols to worship and trust – the eternal God who made you and sent his Son for you. Have you realized that Jesus has done it all: his work on the cross is finished, and all you have to do is receive it by faith? Have you understood the benefits of that: being made right with God, being made a member of his family, having the Spirit sent to live in you? Have you seen that God doesn't expect or want you to put things right on your own, but his Spirit will lead and power you up on a daily basis for the idol busting you so badly want?

### New beginnings

I suspect that you have, and that God has shown you a lot about yourself and about his ways. You are sensing some real movement and change. It feels good. However, it may be that at this point you are feeling torn. All this stuff about idols does make some sense. It definitely explains some things about you which had puzzled you. It does sound as though there is a better way to live. You've got this real sense that you want things to be different.

### Pulled two ways

At the same time, you feel this inner tension, two forces pulling
you in opposite directions. Those idols have got awfully
familiar. They feel part of you. You've lived with them a long
time: you're at home with one another. You've been wired
that way a long time. Though your idols aren't real, there are
spiritual powers out there that use them: they are real and
they will be fighting back. Like advocates arguing with all their
ability in court for a case they know to be bogus, these powers
are using every trick they have to persuade you to stick with
your idols.

### The downward spiral

Perhaps you have tried to break free, but have fallen back into
old ways. Anger breaks out, lust breaks free, your resolutions
are repeatedly broken. Idol busting is a lifelong process. We
don't just repent and rest in Christ and then see everything
change in an instant. It happens gradually over time. Typically,
a habit takes two to three months to lose or form. Of course,
the Holy Spirit can shorten this time and our wobbles can
lengthen it.

We forget this, however. We tend to analyse our idol
problem, try to put ourselves right, but then fail. When we
fail, we feel so bad that we revert to some comfort idol to take
away the sense of shame. Then we feel ashamed again about
the comfort idol and we spiral downwards. There is this
constant bouncing back and forth.

### I'll do it my way

A powerful new idolatrous pattern is taking hold of us: the
idol of self-improvement or, more simply, the idol of self. I
can change myself. I can do it. I want to change myself, then
I can feel good about myself! See the pattern? It's idolatry of

a subtle, plausible and deadly kind. We all have it at some stage and in some form.

### God uses those failures!

Idol busting is a lifelong process with ups and downs along the way. God allows the downs (without excusing them for a moment) in order to make us depend all the more on him and to zap our pride. But we have to accept our own brokenness, not try to put it right ourselves.

### Me, me, me

You see, the danger with any bit of thinking about idolatry is that we see it as being all about us. We can become obsessed with our obsessions and idolatrous in our idol busting, turning from sin to self-righteousness, a much more subtle kind of idolatry! We can navel-gaze. I know all too well from experience how easy it is to make ourselves our great obsession as we probe for insight and understanding of how we are wired and where our idols lead us astray.

This is itself idolatrous because the focus is on me, not Christ. We can set to work to save ourselves. One way in which this shows in my life is when I don't work on my idols out of a conscious sense of dependence on the leading and help of the Spirit. I am a rationalistic, self-reliant self. I don't need him. Oh yes I do! But I try to be my own deliverer. And the system crashes again like a computer with an ineradicable bug in the operating system.

### Wanting to be God

Martin Luther wrote that 'Man is by nature unable to want God to be God. Indeed, he himself wants to be God and does not want God to be God.'[5] Are you allowing your new insights into idols and a determination to be your own idol buster to become new ways of being your own god again?

*It's all about you, Jesus*
Your thinking that this book is about you is perhaps a sign that you, like me, are still far too me-centred. It is a sign of vanity and self-centredness, which are symptoms of idolatry. We have been working towards self-knowledge. That is very different from self-centredness because self-knowledge leads us to focus on God and other people.

This book isn't about you! Forgive me if an excess of personal references have made it too much about me. It isn't about either of us, because life isn't about either of us: it is about God. It is about his eternal being in three persons in love, joy and glory, his creation, his plan, his rightful place on the throne of the universe and the altar of our hearts. He is out to recapture those hearts. How far have you allowed him to get with yours?

> Holy Spirit, all divine,
> Dwell within this heart of mine
> Cast down every idol throne
> Reign supreme, reign alone.[6]

## For discussion or personal reflection
Read Philippians 3:1–14.

1. Paul talks about 'confidence in the flesh'. How do your efforts to get rid of your idols feel like putting confidence in something other than Christ and the power of the Holy Spirit?
2. What do you see in verses 8–11 which encourage you in your battle against idolatry?

3. How do verses 12–14 speak to us when we feel we aren't making any progress?

4. List the three most important things you have gained from this book.

   a) _____

   b) _____

   c) _____

5. What would your life look like in a year's time if God's plan to recapture your heart continues in the power of the Holy Spirit?

6. What can you do to help that process along:

- in your home?
- in your work?
- in your neighbourhood?
- in your church?
- in your closest relationships?
- in your use of time?

7. Spend some time thanking God for what he has shown you and asking him to make that better future real in your life.

## Further spiritual exercise

Has something in this book touched your heart? Perhaps it has reawakened your hunger for God? Why not take the words of this hymn by William Cowper and work through them in prayerful meditation.

> O! for a closer walk with God,
> A calm and heavenly frame;
> Light to shine upon the road
> That leads me to the Lamb!

Do you long for a closer walk with God? Remind yourself of all the reasons why.

> Where is the blessedness I knew
> When first I saw the Lord?
> Where is the soul-refreshing view
> Of Jesus and his word?

Recall a time when your soul was refreshed by Jesus though his word. Go back to it in the imagination of your memory. Would you like that again?

> What peaceful hours I once enjoyed!
> How sweet their memory still!
> But they have left an aching void,
> The world can never fill.

How have you been trying to fill your inner void with the 'world'? Has it worked?

> Return, O holy Dove, return!
> Sweet the messenger of rest!
> I hate the sins that made thee mourn
> And drove thee from my breast.

Can you get yourself back to God? Or do you need him to come back to you? Load your mind with the horror, the insanity, the insult of your sins. Ask him to fill you instead.

> The dearest idol I have known,
> Whate'er that idol be,
> Help me to tear it from thy throne,
> And worship only thee.

What is your dearest idol? Ask Jesus to help you remove it from his rightful place.

> So shall my walk be close with God,
> Calm and serene my frame;
> So purer light shall mark the road
> That leads me to the Lamb.

Rest confidently in Christ.

# FURTHER READING

Elyse Fitzpatrick, *Idols of the Heart: Learning to Live for God Alone* (Presbyterian and Reformed, 2001). Practical, pastoral and, I suspect, especially helpful for women.

Bob Goudzwaard, *Idols of Our Time* (IVP, 1984). Out of print and a little dated, but still masterly in identifying contemporary political idolatry.

Dick Keyes, *Beyond Identity: Finding Yourself in the Image and Character of God* (Wipf and Stock, 1998). Intellectually stimulating and very practical.

C. John Miller, *Repentance: A Daring Call to Real Surrender* (CLC Publications, 2009). Practical and challenging.

Vinoth Ramachandra, *Gods that Fail: Modern Idolatry and Christian Mission* (Paternoster, 1996). Another intellectual analysis: very powerful.

Brian Rosner, *How to Get Really Rich: A Sharp Look at the Religion of Greed* (IVP, 1999) – it is still available second hand, and very helpful.

# NOTES

## Introduction
1 Not that I am suggesting for a moment that you have garden gnomes.
2 'Man's nature is a perpetual factory of idols' (John Calvin, *Institutes of the Christian Religion*, trans. Ford Lewis Battles, The Westminster Press, 1960, I: xi.8).
3 From 'Walking with God' by William Cowper.

## Chapter 1
1 Martin Luther, *The Large Catechism*, http://www.bookofconcord.org/lc-3-tencommandments.php, accessed 28 September 2009.
2 David Clarkson, 'Soul Idolatry Excludes Men out of Heaven', a sermon on Ephesians 5:5 available at www.gracegems.org/SERMONS/Clarkson_soul_idolatry.htm, accessed 26 July 2006. Recommended by Brian Rosner, in *How to Get Really Rich: A Sharp Look at the Religion of Greed* (IVP, 1999), pp. 55–57.
3 Simon Barnes, *The Times*, 2 July 2008.
4 Tim Keller teaches this distinction, which has huge explanatory power.
5 I owe this to Jenny Dorsey who, I believe, adapted it from unpublished material from Tim Keller.
6 I am deeply grateful to Tim Chester, who kept repeating this phrase at our fraternal meetings in explanation of all sorts of things, like why we don't pray more. See also George Marsden, *Jonathan Edwards: A Life* (Yale University Press, 2003), pp. 440–441, for a more theological rationale for this as a summary of Jonathan Edwards' teaching on the Freedom of the Will.
7 Albert Ellis, quoted by Gerard Egan, *The Skilled Helper: A Problem-Management and Opportunity Development Approach to Helping* (8th ed., Brooks/Cole, 2008), p. 141.
8 I got the idea for this from Jenny Dorsey, who in turn, I believe, adapted it from Tim Keller.
9 Sadly there is no prospect of this or any other book being printed at HWV now. The company closed in the 1990s and the land is now occupied by a supermarket.
10 The fact that I can still remember the price from way back in 1986 shows how much it meant to me!
11 Taken from unpublished material shared.
12 Thanks to the anonymous IVP reader who pointed this out.

## Chapter 2
1 Particularly in finding someone to sleep with!
2 Albert Ellis, *How to Stubbornly Refuse to Make Yourself Miserable about Anything – Yes, Anything* (Citadel Press, 2006), p. 14.
3 Ibid., p. 13.

4 Dave Harvey, *When Sinners Say 'I Do': Discovering the Power of the Gospel for Marriage* (Shepherd Press, 2007), p. 74.

5 J. John, quoted in Guy Brandon, *Just Sex: Is It Ever Just Sex?* (IVP, 2009), p. 85.

6 'Have' means 'have sex with' in this verse.

7 Quoted by John Stott, in *The Message of 1 Timothy and Titus,* The Bible Speaks Today series (IVP, 1996), p. 115. For more on this theme see the chapter 'Enjoying God's gifts' in my book *Maximum Life* (IVP, 2009), where this quotation is repeated.

## Chapter 3

1 Frank Thielman, *The NIV Application Commentary: Philippians* (Zondervan, 1995), pp. 243–244.

2 Cyprian, Epistle 1:12, quoted in Brian Rosner, *How to Get Really Rich: A Sharp Look at the Religion of Greed* (IVP, 1999).

3 Tom Wright, *Hebrews for Everyone* (SPCK, 2003), on Hebrews 13:4–6.

4 Carl Trueman, at http://www.reformation21.org/Past_Issues/ 2006_Issues_1_16_/2006_Issues_1_16_Counterpoints/Zen_Calvinism/224/.

5 It doesn't seem unfair to name and shame the paper in question as *The Times*, once a rather restrained publication.

6 C. S. Lewis, *Mere Christianity*, Fiftieth Anniversary Edition (HarperCollins, 2002), p. 86. Thanks to Ray Ortlund for this quote.

7 Jeremiah Burroughs.

8 Anonymous prayer in Arthur Bennet, *The Valley of Vision: A Collection of Puritan Prayers and Devotions* (Banner of Truth, 1975), p. 51.

9 Donald Macleod, *From Glory to Golgotha* (Christian Focus Publications, 2002), p. 155.

10 Testimony at Eden Baptist Church, February 2009.

11 Thanks to Kate Byrom for suggesting this point.

## Chapter 4

1 As C. S. Lewis suggests somewhere.

2 The relative clause 'such a person is an idolater' refers grammatically to the covetous person.

3 Peter T. O'Brien, *The Letter to the Ephesians, Pillar New Testament Commentary* (Apollos, 1999), pp. 362–363.

4 D. J. Atkinson and D. H. Fields (eds.), *New Dictionary of Christian Ethics and Pastoral Theology* (IVP, 1995).

5 From a sermon by Peter Lewis on Romans 1, available at http://www. cornerstoneuk.org.uk/resources/archive/results.php?selection= Romans&id=1.

6 This is not a bit of reactionary exaggeration. I have lost count of the number of times *The Times*, my newspaper of choice, has a banner headline in colour along the very top of the front page with the word 'sex' in it, often relating to a short and marginal article in some minor part of the paper that day.

7 See Guy Brandon, *Just Sex: Is It Ever Just Sex?* (IVP, 2009).

8 Personal Health and Social Education.

9 It's interesting how often emptiness is connected with idolatry, isn't it?

10 Al Martin's phrase in a memorable sermon on sexual purity to young people in Leicester in 1984.

11 From public baptism testimonies in 2006 at Eden Baptist Church.

12 Many thanks to the friend who wrote this and agreed I could include it here.

13 Peter Hicks suggests twelve steps to break free from sexual sin in *What Could I Say? A Handbook for Helpers* (IVP, 2000), pp. 244–245. Available as a downloadable document from www.eden-cambridge.org.

14 Jonathan Berry, *True Freedom Trust News*, December 2008.

## Chapter 5

1 Michelle Graham, *Wanting To Be Her: Body Image Secrets Victoria Won't Tell You* (IVP, 2004), pp. 47–48.

2 Not my no. 1 reading normally, I assure you . . .

3 Naomi Wolf, *The Beauty Myth* (Anchor/Doubleday, 1991), pp. 246–248.

4 Lillian Calles Barger, *Eve's Revenge: Women and a Spirituality of the Body* (Brazos, 2003), pp. 44–45.

5 Graham, *Wanting to Be Her*, p. 16.

6 Barger, *Eve's Revenge*, pp. 47–48.

7 Wolf, *The Beauty Myth*, pp. 82–84.

8 Ibid., p. 62.

9 Ibid., pp. 185–186.

10 http://www.harleymedical.co.uk/cosmetic-surgery-for-women/breast-surgery/breast-enlargement-implants-and-augmentation/, accessed 28 April 2009.

11 http://www.harleymedical.co.uk/cosmetic-surgery-for-women/breast-surgery/breast-enlargement-implants-and-augmentation/?document_id=164, accessed 28 April 2009.

12 http://www.harleymedical.co.uk/cosmetic-surgery-for-men/the-face/faceneck-lift-rhytidectomy/, accessed 28 April 2009.

13 Wolf, *The Beauty Myth*, p. 231.

14 Barger, *Eve's Revenge*, pp. 172–173.

15 Thanks to Dr Bruce Winter for this anecdote.

16 Graham, *Wanting To Be Her*, p. 148.

17 Ibid.

18 John Stott, *The Message of 1 Timothy and Titus*, The Bible Speaks Today series (IVP, 1996), on 1 Timothy 3.

19 For more on this, see chapter 4 on 'Lust'.

20 Graham, *Wanting To Be Her*, p. 147.

## Chapter 6

1 Many thanks to Amy Donovan for this bizarre information.

2 Thanks to the fellow walker I met on the summit of Cadair Idris who gave me both chocolate and advice: to include a section on celebrity worship in this book.

3  Oliver O'Donovan, *The Ways of Judgment* (Alban Books, 2005), pp. 159–160. Much of this discussion is indebted to his analysis of celebrity.

4  See Christopher Ash's powerful little book, *Listen Up! A Practical Guide to Listening to Sermons* (Good Book Company, 2009).

5  Simon Walker, *Leading Out of Who You Are: Discovering the Art of Undefended Leadership* (Piquant, 2007), p. 16. He goes on to analyse in an amazingly accurate way the inner and outer lives of a well-known English evangelical preacher who was idolized by many and came to grief morally in the 1990s.

6  His biographer suggests that at times Robbie seems to be 'a needy, insecure, contradictory egomaniac who would like to be loved and prefer to be left alone exactly at the times and in the proportions that suit him' (Chris Heath, *Feel: Robbie Williams*, Ebury Press, 2004, p. 7). A book to be read with discernment, if at all.

7  *The Works of John Newton* (Banner of Truth, 1988), vol. 6, pp. 268–269.

8  Michelle Graham, *Wanting To Be Her: Body Image Secrets Victoria Won't Tell You* (IVP, 2004), pp. 96–97.

9  Herman Hendrix, *Getting the Love You Need* (Pocket Books, 2005), p. 158.

10  *The Works of John Newton*, vol. 6, pp. 268–269.

11  Ibid., vol. 2, letter IV.

12  Thanks to my wife Debbie for this acute observation.

## Chapter 7

1  Thanks to Rohintan Mody, who pointed this out to me.

2  Rohintan Mody, *The Relationship between Powers of Evil and Idols in 1 Corinthians 8:4–5 and 10:18–22 in the Context of the Pauline Corpus and Early Judaism* (unpublished PhD thesis, University of Aberdeen, 2008).

3  For further reading on this topic, see Fong Yang Wong, *Freedom and Consideration: The Christian's Dilemma Concerning Food Offered to Idols* (Pustaka Sufes, 1994); Daniel Tong, *A Biblical Approach to Chinese Traditions and Beliefs* (Armour, 2003). Thanks to Marvin Wong, who recommended these titles.

4  A. W. Tozer, *The Knowledge of the Holy* (STL, 1976), p. 11.

5  I reject the distinction between 'secular' and 'sacred' work, between Christian activities and non-Christian ones. Biblically the whole of life is lived to the glory of God (see my book *Maximum Life*, IVP, 2009). However, I adopt this ultimately false distinction for the sake of the argument here.

6  Not because I use a strange calendar, but because I take Monday as a 'day off'.

7  Ruth Tucker, *From Jerusalem to Irian Jaya: A Biographical History of Christian Missions* (Academie, 1983), p. 469.

8  Ibid., p. 470.

9  Ibid., p. 471.

10  For more on this, see Matthew Elliott, *Faithful Feelings* (IVP, 2006).

## Chapter 8

1　It is arguably one of the critical weaknesses in the brilliant and powerful book by Jeffrey Sachs, *The End of Poverty: How We Can Make It Happen in Our Lifetime* (Penguin, 2005), notably in his argument for massive international aid for developing nations. He downplays the effects of worldview, culture and corruption in holding poor countries back. Thanks to Steve Bryan for this insight.

2　See, for instance, the thoughtful and ingenious books by Paul Collier (OUP, 2007), and *Wars, Guns and Votes: Democracy in Dangerous Places* (Bodley Head, 2009), and the provocative, maverick *The White Man's Burden* (OUP, 2001) by William Easterly, which exposes the fallacies of externally imposed plans and pleads for trial and error. However, in not acknowledging God, each of these also tends in the end to the idolatrous.

3　Not North Korea, though.

4　David Wells, *Above All Earthly Pow'rs* (IVP, 2006), pp. 39–40.

5　Bronwen Maddox, the newspaper's foreign affairs editor, writing in *The Times*, 6 November 2008.

6　Bob Goudzwaard, *Idols of Our Time* (IVP, 1984), p. 47.

7　Eberhard Busch, *Karl Barth, His Life from Letters and Autobiographical Texts*, trans. John Bowden (SCM, 1976), pp. 218, 223, 224.

8　Goudzwaard, *Idols of Our Time*, p. 73.

9　Not that it made much difference, or that I thought it would, in case you fear I suffer from delusions of grandeur.

10　Not really! Thanks to Amy Donovan for her witty observation on a spelling mistake in one of my emails.

11　It also has a whiff of hypocrisy about it: a majority of people in the UK would inflate an insurance or expenses claim if they could do so undetected. The University of Westminster did a survey of company directors which showed that the vast majority would break the law if they thought they could get away with it.

12　Oliver O'Donovan, *The Ways of Judgment* (Alban Books, 2005), p. 171.

13　'Money is the alienated essence of man's labour and life and this alien essence dominates him as he worships it' (quoted in Brian Rosner, *Greed as Idolatry*, Eerdmans, 2007, p. 20).

14　Vinoth Ramachandra, *Gods that Fail: Modern Idolatry and Christian Mission* (Paternoster, 1996), p. 48.

15　John Gray, *Heresies: Against Progress and Other Illusions* (Granta, 2004), p. 6.

16　Wells, *Above All Earthly Pow'rs*, p. 25.

17　Gray, *Heresies*, p. 6.

18　Evolution may or may not be scientifically true, and may or may not as a scientific theory collide irreconcilably with biblical faith. Without endorsing every jot and tittle, I have been stimulated on this by Denis Alexander's work, including *Creation or Evolution? Do We Have to Choose?* (Monarch 2008). He argues that we don't.

19　Dr J. Budziszewski, *Escape from Nihilism*, http://www.leaderu.com/real/ri9801/budziszewski.html.

20  As the poet John Keats claimed, and as the nineteenth-century writer and critic Walter Pater developed into the ideology of aestheticism.
21  Actually it wasn't the whole of English literature, but a few select poets and novelists, chosen by Leavis himself.

## Chapter 9
1  Hence the 'Laws of Strange Worship' in the post-biblical Jewish writings known as the Mishnah.
2  A great excuse to use the Microsoft Word Thesaurus for the first time. Thanks, Bill!
3  We will think more about God's jealousy in chapter 10.
4  For evidence that the Israelites worshipped idols in Egypt, see Joshua 24:14.
5  See http://www.independent.co.uk/news/obituaries/donald-regan-548278.html, accessed 18 May 2009.
6  See, for example, http://www.dailymail.co.uk/home/you/article-1018095/Rita-Rogers-Diana-immensely-proud-sons.html, accessed 18 May 2009.
7  'Idols', in David Freedman (ed.), *Anchor Bible Dictionary* (Yale University Press, 1992), vol. 3, p. 377.
8  Ibid., p. 378.
9  John Walton, *Ancient Near Eastern Thought and the Old Testament: Introducing the Conceptual World of the Hebrew Bible* (Apollos, 2007), p. 116.
10  John Mackay, *Jeremiah: A Mentor Commentary* (Christian Focus Publications, 2004), vol. I, p. 507.
11  Unbelievably, the rarest card, depicting an animal called 'Charizard', reached a price of £60 second-hand on the internet.
12  The same idea is in Psalm 106:20 and Hosea 4:7.
13  These three ideas are all from Greg Beale, *We Become What We Worship: A Biblical Theology of Idolatry* (Apollos, 2009), p. 222.
14  The words translated 'image' and 'likeness' are also used for idols in other parts of the Old Testament.
15  I am grateful to John Richardson, who helped me to see this more clearly in a lecture at Eden Baptist Church in April 2009.
16  Jacques Ellul, quoted in Paul D. Murray, 'Theology "Under the Lash"', in Stephen C. Barton (ed.), (T. & T. Clark, 2007), p. 255.

## Chapter 10
1  Oh yes he is!
2  Thanks to Stuart Doyle for this and many other 'Bobsessive' gems.
3  Walter Eichrodt, quoted in K. Erik Thoennes, *Godly Jealousy: A Theology of Intolerant Love* (Christian Focus Publications, 2005), p. 7. Thanks to Erik for giving me a copy of his powerful study.
4  To find this theme unpacked and explained at length, see John Piper, *Desiring God: Meditations of a Christian Hedonist* (IVP, 1988).
5  Thanks to Drs Clare Gribbin and Yin Ling Woo for medical advice on this point.

6  Kate Fox, *Watching the English: The Hidden Rule of English Behaviour* (Hodder & Stoughton, 2004), p. 52. Essential reading for English and non-English people alike if you want to understand what makes us tick. I discovered all sorts of things about myself and other English people through reading it . . .
7  Tom Wright, *Luke for Everyone* (SPCK, 2004), pp. 231–232.

## Chapter 11
1  Apologies to anyone not covered by these possibilities.
2  Ian Provan, in *Ex Auditu* (1999), p. 29.
3  New American Standard Bible.
4  Greg Beale, *We Become What We Worship: A Biblical Theology of Idolatry* (Apollos, 2009).
5  Walter Brueggemann, *A Commentary on Jeremiah: Exile and Homecoming* (Eerdmans, 1998), p. 34.
6  Provan, *Ex Auditu*, p. 28.
7  C. P. Snow, *The Masters* (Penguin, 1951), p. 212.
8  Jonathan Aitken, *Pride and Perjury: The Rise and Fall of a Political Giant* (HarperCollins, 2000), pp. 8–9.
9  Thanks to Peter Lewis, who shared this quote with me.
10  Again, I owe this quote to Peter Lewis.
11  *Daily Express*, 31 October 1972. Again, via Peter Lewis.
12  Harry Blamires, *The Christian Mind* (SPCK, 1963), p. 103.
13  I mean, by this, a conscious everlasting experience of being destroyed. I cannot imagine it.

## Chapter 12
1  In the Jeeves novels by P. G. Wodehouse.
2  I learned this pattern – Repentance, Forgiveness, Adoption and the Holy Spirit – from the Sonship Course, distributed by World Harvest Mission.
3  C. John Miller, *Repentance: A Daring Call to Real Surrender* (CLC Publications, 2009), p. 11.
4  I am not sure if Jack Miller got this idea from Tim Keller, or vice versa, but I am sure it is true!
5  Out of that experience came his book, *Repentance* (see pp. 11, 94).
6  I got this great phrase from a powerful sermon on Romans 5 preached at Eden Baptist Church by David Field in 2005.
7  Edward T. Welch, *When People Are Big and God Is Small: Overcoming Peer Pressure, Codependency and the Fear of Man* (Presbyterian and Reformed, 1997), p. 113.

## Chapter 13
1  J. I. Packer, *Knowing God* (Hodder & Stoughton, 1993), p. 233.
2  The section that follows is indebted to Peter Lewis.
3  Peter Lewis, unpublished sermon.
4  Ibid.

5  Packer, *Knowing God*, p. 254.
6  The section that follows was prompted by listening to the Sonship Course produced by World Harvest Mission.
7  Some of my socks have days of the week printed on them and sometimes, very occasionally, I even wear the right ones on the right days.
8  Jeannette Bakke, *Holy Invitations: Exploring Spiritual Direction* (Baker, 2000), pp. 164–165.

## Chapter 14

1  Tim Keller – unpublished material.
2  Lois Mowday, *The Snare: Avoiding Emotional and Sexual Entanglements* (NavPress, 1988), p. 75. She goes on to acknowledge that God does use other people to comfort us when we are low or vulnerable. It is the excessive demand for such comfort or reliance on it that is idolatrous. There is an excellent section on this distinction in Dave Harvey, *When Sinners Say 'I Do': Discovering the Power of the Gospel for Marriage* (Shepherd Press, 2007).
3  To borrow Thomas Hobbes's famous phrase.
4  John Piper's phrase. For a great guide to joy, try Mike Mason, *Champagne for the Soul: Rediscovering God's Gift of Joy* (Regent College, 2003).
5  See Raymond C. Ortlund Jr, *Supernatural Living for Natural People: Studies in Romans Eight* (Christian Focus Publications, 2001), pp. 163–164.
6  'Because Jesus lives forever, he has a permanent priesthood. Therefore he is able to save completely those who come to God through him, because he always lives to intercede for them' (Hebrews 7:24–25).
7  I owe this illustration to Os Guinness, *The Call* (Word, 2003), p. 45. Later in life, unfortunately, Coltrane's faith seemed to veer away from the Bible into pantheism.

## Chapter 15

1  From 'Fellowship with the Father', Sonship Course, Lecture 6, published by World Harvest Mission.

## Chapter 16

1  Covered rather well in the movie *Shrek* by a group called Smash Mouth. The original line was 'Then I saw *her* face.'
2  My favourite.
3  Thanks to Greg Beale, *We Become What We Worship: A Biblical Theology of Idolatry* (Apollos, 2009), p. 219, for this connection.
4  David Robertson, *Awakening: The Life and Ministry of Robert Murray McCheyne* (Paternoster, 2004), p. 92. Well worth reading.
5  Thanks to Rosemary Drew and Amy Donovan for reminding me of this.

## Chapter 17

1  John Owen, *Works* (Banner of Truth Trust, 1965), vol. 9, pp. 112–130.

2 'He has shown all you people what is good. And what does the Lord require of you? To act justly and to love mercy and *to walk humbly* with your God' (Micah 6:8, emphasis mine).
3 A phrase I have borrowed from David Field.
4 *The Letters of Samuel Rutherford* (Banner of Truth, 1984), Letter LXX.
5 Michelle Graham, *Wanting To Be Her: Body Image Secrets Victoria Won't Tell You* (IVP, 2004), pp. 14–15.
6 Pablo Martinez, *A Thorn in the Flesh: Finding Strength and Hope Amid Suffering* (IVP, 2007), p. 89.
7 Mike Mason, *Practising the Presence of People: How We Learn to Love* (Waterbrook, 1999), pp. 40–41.
8 Peter Lewis, *The Lord's Prayer: The Greatest Prayer in the World* (Paternoster, 2008), p. 184.

## Chapter 18
1 Charles Spurgeon points this out in a sermon on Jeremiah 33:9. He goes on to say that there would be something rather monstrous about undiluted joy in this life if we had no sadness over our sins, no compassion for human suffering, no outrage at offence to the glory of God, no anger at injustice, etc.
2 Octavius Winslow, *No Condemnation in Christ Jesus* (Banner of Truth, 1991), p. 204.

## Chapter 19
1 Though Warren Beatty heads the list of suspects.
2 'The Promised Land' by Bruce Springsteen from the bleak *Darkness on the Edge of Town* album. Copyright © 1978 Bruce Springsteen (ASCAP). Reprinted by permission. International copyright secured. All rights reserved.
3 Quoted in Dick Keyes, *Beyond Identity: Finding Yourself in the Image and Character of God* (Wipf and Stock, 1998), p. 99.
4 Don't forget that in the Bible the 'heart' means our inner being with its thought and imagination and inclinations. These are closely tied to our emotions, but are not limited to them.
5 Martin Luther, *Disputation against Scholastic Theology*, Thesis 17.
6 From 'Holy Ghost, Light Divine' by Andrew Reed, a Congregational minister in the nineteenth century. His church in east London saw astonishing numbers of people become Christians through his preaching and the power of the Holy Spirit. He had a great heart and vision for the needy and the vulnerable. Taking the lead again and again, he oversaw special homes for orphans and people with special needs for whom no-one else would care. You can read his story in a gripping book: Ian Shaw, *The Greatest is Charity – The Life of Andrew Reed, Preacher and Philanthropist* (Evangelical Press, 2005).